ALEXANDER HAMILTON

Adultery and Apology

ALEXANDER HAMILTON

Adultery and Apology

OBSERVATIONS ON
CERTAIN DOCUMENTS
IN THE HISTORY
OF THE UNITED STATES
FOR THE YEAR 1796

BY ALEXANDER HAMILTON

ALEXANDER HAMILTON,
LATE SECRETARY OF THE TREASURY,
IS FULLY REFUTED.
WRITTEN BY HIMSELF.

Racehorse Publishing

Visit our website at www.skyhorsepublishing.com.

10 9 8 7 6 5 4 3 2 1

Cover design by Michael Short
Cover photographs: iStockphoto

Print ISBN: 978-1-63158-167-0
Ebook ISBN: 978-1-63158-168-7

Printed in the United States of America

FOREWORD

Shocker!

It was a shocker! News of the publication spread far and wide, sparking gossip and disbelief among both the general public and the political class. By his own hand, the secretary of the treasury, Alexander Hamilton, had admitted in print the sordid details of his sexual affair with a married woman. The Founding Father and hero of the Revolutionary War had hoped his lengthy pamphlet written with forthright candor and in vivid prose would nullify the charges of financial misconduct being leveled against him. But rather than defending his character, the infamous essay ended up being his undoing. Not only was it one of the first highly public sex scandals in America, but the affair marked the beginning of the end of Hamilton's political power. Yet, this unusual and fascinating publication offers a window into both the temperament of the man at the center of the maelstrom and the state of political intrigue in the early days of the new republic.

It all started with a surprise visit by a twenty-three-year-old woman named Maria Reynolds. The attractive blond showed up one summer day in 1791 at Hamilton's residence in Philadelphia distressed and begging for help. He was, at the time, thirty-four and serving as the secretary of the treasury in George Washington's Administration. As she told it, her husband, James Reynolds, was abusive and had departed the city and abandoned her. Now destitute, the tearful Mrs. Reynolds needed legal assistance, money, and a place to stay.

The handsome, charismatic politician with a reputation for enjoying the company of attractive, young women happened to also be alone, his wife and children having gone back to their native New York for an extended vacation. Hamilton greeted Mrs. Reynolds but claimed he was busy that day. He did, however, offer his assistance and promised he would obtain the money Maria needed and deliver it later that evening. Foolishly, Hamilton went to the Reynolds residence claiming that nothing "other than pecuniary consolation would be acceptable" to either of them. But they both had other interests. She invited him to join her in the upstairs bedroom and the two began a torrid affair.

The sexual relationship continued through the summer and fall of 1791. However, James Reynolds returned to the city in December. On the fifteenth of the month, Hamilton received an emotional warning from Maria, who wrote in a marginally literate letter, "I have not tim[e] to tell you the cause of my present troubles only that Mr. has [w] rote you this morning and I know not w[h]ether you have got the letter or not and he has swore that If you do not answer It or If he dose not se[e] or hear from you to day he will write Mrs. Hamilton."

In a state of panic, Maria also told Hamilton that her husband had "Gone oute." Noting that she was alone, she begged Hamilton to "Come to her one moment that you May know the Cause then you will the better know how to act." Being caught by her husband appears to have unnerved Maria and prompted concern about her lover's career. She confessed, "Oh my God I feel more for you than myself and wish I had never been born to give you so much unhappiness." Nevertheless, the two continued their affair.

A PROPOSAL AND A PREDICAMENT

The letter from Mr. Reynolds arrived two days later. It charged that the affair had ruined a happy marriage. Of "the injury done me," Reynolds claimed, "there is nothing that you Can do will compensate for it." In the late eighteenth century, it was not uncommon for men embroiled in a lover's triangle to settle matters on the dueling grounds, but Reynolds proposed a different resolution for the predicament. Despite his earlier claim, apparently there was a way to compensate him. Literally. He wrote, "I have this preposial to make to you. [G]ive me the Sum Of thousand dollars and I will le[a]ve the town and take my daughter with me . . . . "

Reynolds played on Hamilton's guilt, baiting him by claiming falsely, "Its true its in your power to do a great deal for me, but its out of your power to do any thing that will Restore to me my Happiness again for if you should give me all you possess would not do it. [G]od knows I love the woman and wish every blessing may attend her, you have bin the Cause of Winning her love, and I Don't think I Can be Reconciled to live with Her . . . " Hamilton paid the bribe.

However, Reynolds did not leave town; nor did Hamilton end the affair. Both matters allowed Reynolds to further entrap the famous Founder. In fact, Mrs. Reynolds appears to have become complicit in the scheme. Maria continued to invite Hamilton to her bed, writing, "With tears in my eyes . . . I shal[l] be miserable till I se[e] you . . . My breast will be in a state of pain and woe." She closed the letter: "P.S. If you cannot come this Evening to stay just come only for one moment as I shal[l] be [a]Lone . . . " Hamilton did not resist. Mr. Reynolds soon began requesting small payments of thirty and forty dollars to guarantee his silence.

The bizarre arrangement may have continued if not for two developments. A professional swindler, Reynolds was also involved in a shady plan to purchase Revolutionary War veterans' pensions. The scheme eventually caught the attention of the law. In November of 1792, he was charged with forgery and jailed. From his cell the opportunistic businessman asked Hamilton for help, but the request was denied. Angry and desperate, Reynolds then informed Hamilton's political opponents of the affair and the arrangement for hush-money payments. The crook even inaccurately insinuated that Hamilton was the source behind the war pension speculation and forgery cabal.

As one of the leaders of the Federalist Party since its inception, Hamilton was an inviting target for Anti-Federalists (also known as the Democratic-Republicans or simply "Republicans"). Sure enough, Republican members of Congress visited Mr. Reynolds in his jail cell and Mrs. Reynolds at her home. Armed with the shocking details of the affair and Reynolds's nefarious claims, two of them—James Monroe and Frederick Muhlenberg—confronted Hamilton with the evidence in December of 1792. They even produced the steamy letters he had written to Maria.

Monroe and Muhlenberg assured Hamilton they would be discrete and, for the time being, the affair remained a secret. But Monroe's mentor was Thomas Jefferson, who happened to also be Hamilton's bitter rival. As the two most influential members of George Washington's cabinet, these two men squared off on nearly every issue, with Hamilton usually besting the secretary of state. Monroe informed Jefferson of the details of the affair. The secretary of state was eager to settle several scores with Hamilton.

In 1797 the story finally broke. The timing was critical— the competition between the two political factions was heating up, Hamilton and Jefferson had recently resigned their cabinet posts, and Jefferson was pursuing the presidency. The embarrassing and damning details of the affair were published by the muckraking newspaperman, Republican attack dog, and Jefferson ally James Thomson Callender. Hamilton was portrayed in the story as a home-wrecker, seducer, and the mastermind behind Reynolds's financial crimes. His career, marriage, and all that he had worked for was in jeopardy.

THE PRIDEFUL ORPHAN

As Lin Manuel Miranda's hit Broadway musical *Hamilton* raps in the opening act, the Founder was the "bastard, orphan, son of a whore, and a Scotsman dropped in the middle of a forgotten spot in the Caribbean." Born on January 11, 1757 (some historical accounts suggest 1755) on the small island of Nevis in the West Indies, Hamilton's upbringing was filled with difficulty, frustration, and tragedy.

As a teenager living in St. Croix, Hamilton's mother, Rachel Fawcett, was pushed into a marriage she never wanted to a Danish-German Jew named Johann Michael Lavien (sometimes listed as Lavine). Lavien appears to have been abusive and the couple suffered financially after he misspent Rachel's inheritance. As the marriage fell apart, a scandal erupted—the young bride was imprisoned for multiple acts of adultery. After being freed, she fled both her marriage and the island. Soon thereafter, she met James Hamilton, a down-on-his-luck Scotsman. The two could never marry, however, because Lavien had not granted Rachel a divorce before fleeing the island amid a debt controversy and women living in the eighteenth century could not legally initiate a divorce. Hamilton moved in with Rachel and the couple had two children out of wedlock. The youngest was Alexander.

James Hamilton abandoned the family when Alexander was only a boy. A few years later in 1768, Rachel succumbed to a disease that swept through the island, leaving young Alexander orphaned and homeless. Stuck on a small island plagued by disease and hurricanes as well as by slavery and pirates, the young boy's future looked bleak. But he was brilliant, pugnacious, and possessed a magnetic personality as well as a gift for oratory and the written word. Therein would be his salvation. When a devastating hurricane hit the islands in 1772, young Alexander penned an article about the disaster. It was written with a poet's vocabulary and the observations of a scientist. The essay caught the attention of newspapers and would eventually help secure his passage to New York in 1773 (some records suggest 1774).

This painful upbringing hardened the teenager, who developed not only the determination to survive and an extraordinary capacity for work, but a proverbial "chip on the shoulder." For all his gifts, Hamilton had an exaggerated sense of pride, one that lacked perspective and bordered on combativeness. He also became increasingly compulsive and reckless. These traits would eventually catch up with him.

Arriving in America, the teenager received a scholarship to King's College (now Columbia) and began writing essays against British rule. When the fighting started, Hamilton volunteered and repeatedly distinguished himself through bravery on the battlefield. He eventually caught the attention of General George Washington. Hamilton was invited to join the commander's staff in 1777, where he rose quickly to the rank of colonel and assisted Washington with every facet of the war, including helping to win the pivotal victory at Yorktown. The ambitious orphan also managed to marry far above his station, wedding

Elizabeth Schuyler, the middle daughter of one of New York's most influential and wealthy men.

He would risk all this in his response to the Maria Reynolds scandal.

THE RESPONSE

Hamilton claimed that Jefferson and Monroe were behind the leaked story about his affair. However, the historical record is not clear, even if Jefferson certainly had the motivation. The year prior, Hamilton savaged the former secretary of state in an essay, noting the incongruity of Jefferson's carefully crafted image as a common man with the reality of his lavish lifestyle. Hamilton wrote, "Simplicity and humility afford but a flimsy veil to the internal evidence of aristocratic splendor, sensuality, and Epicureanism." Indeed, Jefferson had his own well-documented sexual scandals, including one that would soon become the second high profile affair of the young Republic.

Hamilton was now on trial in the court of public opinion. He believed he could dispute the charges and defend himself from the gossip and accusations by writing his own pamphlet. He had, after all, always been able to write himself out of a bind. In the pamphlet, he would apologize and explain his behavior, but also defend his character. Hamilton decided to admit to the sexual affair and bribes to James Reynolds, describing them as an "irregular and indelicate amour." By doing so, he would demonstrate his honesty and honor which, he reasoned, would then allow him to refute what he thought was the far more damaging charge—that he was involved in Reynolds's pension scam.

"This confession," penned Hamilton with his signature flourishing prose, "is not made without a blush. I cannot be the apologist of any vice because the ardor of passion may have made it mine. I can never cease to condemn myself for the pang which it may inflict in a bosom eminently entitled to all my gratitude, fidelity, and love." Yes, his marriage was also on the line. To his beloved Eliza, whom he hurt and embarrassed deeply, he asked forgiveness. The pamphlet also begged mercy from the country he helped to found and loved so. "The public, too, will, I trust, excuse the confession." It did not.

The great Founder's prideful and impulsive response ended up being self-destructive. Republican newspapers and politicians responded with a frenzy of vicious condemnations. Some of his opponents went so far as to assail the character of his loyal and loving wife. As you, the reader, shall discover in the following pages, the length and excruciatingly intimate details of the essay backfired. Hamilton was often a clever and strategic thinking, but the confession was naive and damning.

LEGACY

Maria Reynolds ended up petitioning for a divorce from her husband. It was Aaron Burr, Hamilton's other political rival, who took the case. As for Hamilton, his fate is well known. Years of disagreements with Burr ended with Hamilton writing a public rebuke of his rival. Burr responded with the challenge of a duel. Once again, Hamilton would pay dearly for his words. On July 11, 1804 in Weehawken, New Jersey, Burr shot Hamilton during the duel. The Founder who had overcome so much and risen to such heights died the next day of his wounds. Hamilton was only forty-seven.

His was an extraordinary and unlikely life of accomplishment—General Washington's most trusted aide, hero of the Revolutionary War, successful attorney, influential delegate to the Constitutional Convention, author of the majority of the Federalist Papers, secretary of the treasury, architect of the nation's financial system, and much more. Yet, a sexual affair that may have denied him the presidency along with his own pride ended his life in a manner befitting a Shakespearean tragedy.

Elizabeth Hamilton, who had long before forgiven her husband, lived another half century. Thanks to her vigilance, his voluminous written record survives, including a touching and prescient letter he penned to her on Independence Day, just one week before his death: "Fly to the bosom of your God and be comforted. With my last idea, I shall cherish the sweet hope of meeting you in a better world. Adieu best of wives and best of Women. Embrace all my darling Children for me."

Robert P. Watson, Ph.D. has published forty books and hundreds of scholarly articles, book chapters, and reference essays on topics in politics and history. He is Professor of American Studies at Lynn University in Florida and a frequent commentator for numerous media outlets around the United States and internationally.

APOLOGY AND ADULTERY

THE SPIRIT OF JACOBINISM, if not entirely a new spirit, has at least been cloathed with a more gigantic body and armed with more powerful weapons than it ever before possessed. It is perhaps not too much to say, that it threatens more extensive and complicated mischiefs to the world than have hitherto flowed from the three great scourges of mankind, WAR, PESTILENCE and FAMINE. To what point it will ultimately lead society, it is impossible for human foresight to pronounce; but there is just ground to apprehend that its progress may be marked with calamities of which the dreadful incidents of the French revolution afford a very faint image. Incessantly busy in undermining all the props of public security and private happiness, it seems to threaten the political and moral world with a complete overthrow.

A principal engine, by which this spirit endeavours to accomplish its purposes is that of calumny. It is essential to its success that the influence of men of upright principles, disposed and able to resist its enterprises, shall be at all events destroyed. Not content with traducing their best efforts for the public good, with misrepresenting their purest motives, with inferring criminality from actions innocent or laudable, the most direct falsehoods are invented and propagated with undaunted effrontery and unrelenting perseverance. Lies often detected and refuted are still revived and repeated, in the hope that the refutation may have been forgotten, or that the frequency and boldness of accusation may supply the place of truth and proof. The most profligate men are encouraged, probably bribed, certainly with patronage if not with money, to become informers and accusers. And when tales, which their characters alone ought to discredit, are refuted by evidence and facts which oblige the patrons of them to abandon their support, they still continue in corroding whispers to wear away the reputations which they could not directly subvert. If, luckily for the conspirators against honest fame, any little foible or folly can be traced out in one, whom they desire to persecute, it becomes at once in their hands a two-edged sword, by which to wound the public character and stab the private felicity of the person. With such men, nothing is sacred. Even the peace of an unoffending and amiable wife is a welcome repast to their insatiate fury against the husband.

In the gratification of this baleful spirit, we not only

hear the jacobin news-papers continually ring with odious insinuations and charges against many of our most virtuous citizens; but, not satisfied with this, a measure new in this country has been lately adopted to give greater efficacy to the system of defamation— periodical pamphlets issue from the same presses, full freighted with misrepresentation and falsehood, artfully calculated to hold up the opponents of the FACTION to the jealousy and distrust of the present generation and if possible, to transmit their names with dishonor to posterity. Even the great and multiplied services, the tried and rarely equaled virtues of a WASHINGTON, can secure no exemption.

How then can I, with pretensions every way inferior expect to escape? And if truly this be, as every appearance indicates, a conspiracy of vice against virtue, ought I not rather to be flattered, that I have been so long and so peculiarly an object of persecution? Ought I to regret, if there be any thing about me, so formidable to the Faction as to have made me worthy to be distinguished by the plenitude of its rancour and venom?

It is certain that I have had a pretty copious experience of its malignity. For the honor of human nature, it is to be hoped that the examples are not numerous of men so greatly calumniated and persecuted as I have been, with so little cause.

I dare appeal to my immediate fellow citizens of whatever political party for the truth of the assertion, that no man ever carried into public life a more unblemished pecuniary reputation, than that with which I undertook the office of Secretary of the Treasury; a character marked by an indifference to the acquisition of property rather than by an avidity for it.

With such a character, however natural it was to expect criticism and opposition, as to the political principles which I might manifest or be supposed to entertain, as to the wisdom or expediency of the plans, which I might propose, or as to the skill, care or diligence with which the business of my department might be executed, it was not natural to expect nor did I expect that my fidelity or integrity in a pecuniary sense, would ever be called in question.

But on this head a mortifying disappointment has been experienced. Without the slightest foundation, I have been repeatedly held up to the suspicions of the world as a man directed in his administration by the most sordid views; who did not scruple to sacrifice the public to his private interest, his duty and honor to the sinister accumulation of wealth.

Merely because I *retained* an opinion once common to me and the most influential of those who opposed me, *That the public debt ought to be provided for on the basis of the contract upon which it was created*, I have been wickedly accused with wantonly increasing the public burthen many millions, in order to promote a stock-jobbing interest of myself and friends.

Merely because a member of the House of

Representatives entertained a different idea from me, as to the legal effect of appropriation laws, and did not understand accounts, I was exposed to the imputation of having committed a deliberate and criminal violation of the laws and to the suspicion of being a defaulter for millions; so as to have been driven to the painful necessity of calling for a formal and solemn inquiry.

The inquiry took place. It was conducted by a committee of fifteen members of the House of Representatives—a majority of them either my decided political enemies or inclined against me, some of them the most active and intelligent of my opponents, without a single man, who being known to be friendly to me, possessed also such knowledge and experience of public affairs as would enable him to counteract injurious intrigues. Mr. Giles of Virginia who had commenced the attack was of the committee.

The officers and hooks of the treasury were examined. The transactions between the several banks and the treasury were scrutinized. Even my *private accounts* with those institutions were laid open to the committee; and every possible facility given to the inquiry. The result was a complete demonstration that the suspicions which had been entertained were groundless.

Those which had taken the fastest hold were, that the public monies had been made subservient to loans, discounts, and accommodations to myself and friends. The committee in reference to this point reported thus:—"It appears from the affidavits of the Cashier and several officers of the bank of the United States and several of the directors, the Cashier, and other officers of the bank of New-York, that the Secretary of the Treasury never has either *directly* or *indirectly*, for himself or any other person, procured any discount or credit from either of the said banks upon the basis of any public monies which at any time have been deposited therein under his direction: And the committee are *satisfied*, that *no monies* of the United States, whether *before* or *after* they have passed to the credit of the Treasurer have ever been *directly* or *indirectly* used for or applied to *any purposes* but those of the government, except so far as all monies deposited in a bank are concerned in the *general operations* thereof."

The report, which I have always understood was unanimous, contains in other respects, with considerable detail the materials of a complete exculpation. My enemies, finding no handle for their malice, abandoned the pursuit.

Yet unwilling to leave any ambiguity upon the point, when I determined to resign my office, I gave early previous notice of it to the House of Representatives, for the declared purpose of affording an opportunity for legislative crimination, if any ground for it had been discovered. Not the least step towards it was taken. From which I have a right to infer the universal conviction of the House, that no cause existed, and to consider the result as a complete vindication.

On another occasion, a worthless man of the name of Fraunces found encouragement to bring forward to the House of Representatives a formal charge against me of unfaithful conduct in office. A Committee of the House was appointed to inquire, consisting in this case also, partly of some of my most intelligent and active enemies.—The issue was an unanimous exculpation of me as will appear by the following extract from the Journals of the House of Representatives of the 19th of February 1794.

> The House resumed the consideration of the report of the Committee, to whom was referred the memorial of Andrew G. Fraunces: whereupon, Resolved, That the reasons assigned by the secretary of the treasury, for refusing payment of the warrants referred to in the memorial, are fully sufficient to justify his conduct; and that in the whole course of this transaction, the secretary and other officers of the treasury, have acted a meritorious part towards the public.
>
> *Resolved,* That the charge exhibited in the memorial, against the secretary of the treasury, relative to the purchase of the pension of Baron de Glaubeck is wholly illiberal and groundless.[1]

---

1. Would it be believed after all this, that Mr. Jefferson, Vice President of the United States would write to this Fraunces friendly letters ? Yet such is the fact as will be seen in the Appendix, Nos. XLIV & XLV.

Was it not to have been expected that these repeated demonstrations of the injustice of the accusations hazarded against me would have abashed the enterprise of my calumniators? However natural such an expectation may seem, it would betray an ignorance of the true character of the Jacobin system. It is a maxim deeply ingrafted in that dark system, that no character, however upright, is a match for constantly reiterated attacks, however false. It is well understood by its disciples, that every calumny makes some proselites and even retains some; since justification seldom circulates as rapidly and as widely as slander. The number of those who from doubt proceed to suspicion and thence to belief of imputed guilt is continually augmenting; and the public mind fatigued at length with resistance to the calumnies which eternally assail it, is apt in the end to sit down with the opinion that a person so often accused cannot be entirely innocent.

Relying upon this weakness of human nature, the Jacobin Scandal-Club though often defeated constantly return to the charge. Old calumnies are served up a-fresh and every pretext is seized to add to the catalogue—The person whom they seek to blacken, by dint of repeated strokes of their brush, becomes a demon in their own eyes, though he might be pure and bright as an angel but for the daubing of those wizard painters.

Of all the vile attempts which have been made to injure my character that which has been lately revived in No. V and VI, of the history of the United States for 1796 is the most vile. This it will be impossible for any *intelligent*, I will not say *candid*, man to doubt, when he shall have accompanied me through the examination.

I owe perhaps to my friends an apology for condescending to give a public explanation. A just pride with reluctance stoops to a formal vindication against so despicable a contrivance and is inclined rather to oppose to it the uniform evidence of an upright character. This would be my conduct on the present occasion, did not the tale seem to derive a sanction from the names of three men of some weight and consequence in the society: a circumstance, which I trust will excuse me for paying attention to a slander that without this prop, would defeat itself by intrinsic circumstances of absurdity and malice.

The charge against me is a connection with one James Reynolds for purposes of improper pecuniary speculation. My real crime is an amorous connection with his wife for a considerable time with his privity and connivance, if not originally brought on by a combination between the husband and wife with the design to extort money from me.

This confession is not made without a blush. I cannot be the apologist of any vice because the ardour of passion may have made it mine. I can never cease to condemn myself for the pang, which it may inflict in a bosom eminently intitled to all my gratitude, fidelity and love. But that bosom will approve, that even at so great an expence, I should effectually wipe away a more serious stain from a name, which it cherishes with no less elevation than tenderness. The public too will I trust excuse the confession. The necessity of it to my defence against a more heinous charge could alone have extorted from me so painful an indecorum.

Before I proceed to an exhibition of the positive proof which repels the charge, I shall analize the documents from which it is deduced, and I am mistaken if with discerning and candid minds more would be necessary. But I desire to obviate the suspicions of the most suspicious.

The first reflection which occurs on a perusal of the documents is that it is morally impossible I should have been foolish as well as depraved enough to employ so vile an instrument as *Reynolds* for such *insignificant ends*, as are indicated by different parts of the story itself—My enemies to be sure have kindly pourtrayed me as another *Chartres* on the score of moral principle. But they have been ever bountiful in ascribing to me talents. It has suited their purpose to exaggerate such as I may possess, and to attribute to them an influence to which they are not intitled. But the present accusation imputes to me as much folly as wickedness—All the documents shew, and it is otherwise matter of notoriety, that Reynolds was an obscure, unimportant and profligate man. Nothing could be more weak, because nothing could be more unsafe than to make use of such an instrument; to use him too without any intermediate agent more worthy of confidence who might keep me out of sight, to write him numerous letters recording the objects of the improper connection (for this is pretended and that the letters were afterwards burnt at my request) to unbosom myself to him with a prodigality of confidence, by very unnecessarily telling him, as he alleges, of a connection in speculation between myself and Mr. Duer. It is very extraordinary, if the head of the money department of a country, being unprincipled enough to sacrifice his trust and his integrity, could not have contrived objects of profit sufficiently large to have engaged the co-operation of men of far greater importance than Reynolds, and with whom there could have been due safety, and should have been driven to the necessity of unkennelling such a reptile to be the instrument of his cupidity.

But, moreover, the scale of the concern with Reynolds, such as it is presented, is contemptibly narrow for a rapacious speculating secretary of the treasury. *Clingman, Reynolds* and his wife were manifestly in very close confidence with each other. It seems there was a free communication of secrets. Yet in clubbing their different items of information as to the supplies of money which Reynolds received from me, what do they amount to? *Clingman* states that Mrs. Reynolds told him, that at a certain time her husband had received from me upwards of eleven hundred dollars. A note is produced which shews that at one time fifty dollars were sent to him, and another note is produced, by which and the information of Reynolds himself through Clingman, it appears that at another time 300 dollars were asked and refused— Another sum of 200 dollars is spoken of by *Clingman*, as having been furnished to Reynolds at some other time. What a scale of speculation is this for the head of a public treasury, for one who in the very publication that brings forward the charge is represented as having procured to be funded at forty millions a debt which ought to have been discharged at ten or fifteen millions for the criminal purpose of enriching himself and his friends? He must have been a clumsy knave, if he did not secure enough of this excess of twenty-five or thirty millions, to have taken away all inducement to risk his character in such bad hands and in so huckstering a way—or to have enabled him, if he did employ such an agent, to do it with more means and to better purpose. It is curious, that this rapacious secretary should at one time have furnished his speculating agent with the paltry sum of fifty dollars, at another, have refused him the inconsiderable sum of 800 dollars, declaring upon his honor that it was not in his power to furnish it. This declaration was true or not; if the last the refusal ill comports with the idea of a speculating connection—if the first, it is very singular that the head of the treasury engaged without scruple in schemes of profit, should have been destitute of so small a sum—But if we suppose this officer to be living upon an inadequate salary, without any collateral pursuits of gain, the appearances then are simple and intelligible enough, applying to them the true key.

It appears that *Reynolds* and *Clingman* were detected by the then comptroller of the treasury, in the odious crime of suborning a witness to commit perjury, for the purpose of obtaining letters of administration on the estate of a person who was living, in order to receive a small sum of money due to him from the treasury—It is certainly extraordinary that the confidential agent of the head of that department should have been in circumstances to induce a resort to so miserable an expedient. It is odd, if there was a speculating connection, that it was not more profitable both to the secretary and to his agent than are indicated by the circumstances disclosed.

It is also a remarkable and very instructive fact, that notwithstanding the great confidence and intimacy, which subsisted between *Clingman*, *Reynolds* and his wife, and which continued till after the period of the liberation of the two former from the prosecution against them, neither of them has ever specified the objects of the pretended connection in speculation between Reynolds and me. The pretext that the letters which contained the evidence were destroyed is no answer. They could not have been forgotten and might have been disclosed from memory. The total omission of this could only have proceeded from the consideration that detail might have led to detection. The destruction of letters besides is a fiction, which is refuted not only by the general improbability, that I should put myself upon paper with so despicable a person on a subject which might expose me to infamy, but by the evidence of extreme caution on my part in this particular, resulting from the laconic and disguised form of the notes which are produced—They prove incontestibly that there was an unwillingness to trust Reynolds with my hand writing. The true reason was that I apprehended he might make use of it to impress upon others the belief of some pecuniary connection with me, and besides implicating my character might render it the engine of a false credit, or turn it to some other sinister use—Hence the disguise; for my conduct in admitting at once and without hesitation that the notes were from me proves that it was never my intention by the expedient of disguising my hand to shelter myself from any serious inquiry.

The accusation against me was never heard of 'till Clingman and Reynolds were under prosecution by the treasury for an infamous crime—It will be seen by the document No. I (a) that during the endeavours of *Clingman* to obtain relief, through the interposition of Mr. Muhlenberg, he made to the latter the communication of my pretended criminality. It will be further seen by document No. II that Reynolds had while in prison conveyed to the ears of Messrs. Monroe and Venable that he could give intelligence of my being concerned in speculation, and that he also supposed that he was kept in prison by a design on my part to oppress him and drive him away. And by his letter to *Clingman* of the 13 of December, after he was released from prison, it also appears that he was actuated by a spirit of revenge against me: for he declares that he will have *satisfaction* from me *at all events*; adding, as addressed to *Clingman*, "And *you only I trust.*"

Three important inferences flow from these circumstances—one that the accusation against me was an auxiliary to the efforts of *Clingman* and *Reynolds* to get released from a disgraceful prosecution—another that there was a vindictive spirit against me at least on the part of Reynolds—the third, that he confided in *Clingman* as a coadjutor in the plan of vengeance.

These circumstances, according to every estimate of the credit due to accusers, ought to destroy their testimony. To what credit are persons intitled, who in telling a story are governed by the double motive of escaping from disgrace and punishment and of gratifying revenge?—As to Mrs. Reynolds, if she was not an accomplice, as it is too probable she was, her situation would naturally subject her to the will of her husband. But enough besides will appear in the sequel to shew that her testimony merits no attention.

The letter which has been just cited deserves a more particular attention—As it was produced by Clingman, there is a chasm of three lines, which lines are manifestly essential to explain the sense. It may be inferred from the context, that these deficient lines would unfold the cause of the resentment which is expressed. 'Twas from them that might, have been learnt the true nature of the transaction. The expunging of them is a violent presumption that they would have contradicted the purpose for which the letter was produced.—A witness offering such a mutilated piece discredits himself. The mutilation is alone satisfactory proof of contrivance and imposition. The manner of accounting for it is frivolous.

The words of the letter are strong—satisfaction is to be had *at all events, per fas et nefas*, and *Clingman* is the chosen confidential agent of the laudable plan of vengeance. It must be confessed he was not wanting in his part.

Reynolds, as will be seen by No. II (a) alleges that a merchant came to him and offered as a volunteer to be his bail, who he suspected had been instigated to it by me, and after being decoyed to the place the merchant wished to carry him to, he refused being his bail, unless he would deposit a sum of money to some considerable amount which he could not do and was in consequence committed to prison. Clingman (No. IV a) tells the same story in substance though with some difference in form leaving to be implied what Reynolds expresses and naming *Henry Seckel* as the merchant. The deposition of this respectable citizen (No. XXIII) gives the lie to both, and shews that he was in fact the agent of *Clingman,* from motives of good will to him, as his former book-keeper, that he never had any communication with me concerning either of them till after they were both in custody, that when he came as a messenger to me from one of them, I not only declined interposing in their behalf, but informed Mr. Seckel that they had been guilty of a crime and advised him to have nothing to do with them.

This single fact goes far to invalidate the whole story. It shews plainly the disregard of truth and the malice by which the parties were actuated. Other important inferences are to be drawn from the transaction. Had I been conscious that I had any thing to fear from *Reynolds* of the nature which has been pretended, should I have warned *Mr. Seckel* against having any thing to do with them? Should I not rather have encouraged him to have come to their assistance? Should I not have been eager to promote their liberation? But this is not the only instance, in which I acted a contrary part. *Clingman* testifies in No. V. that I would not permit *Fraunces* a clerk in my office to become their bail, but signified to him that if he did it, he must quit the department.

Clingman states in No. IV. (a) that my note in answer to Reynolds' application for a loan towards a subscription to the *Lancaster Turnpike* was in his possession from about the time it was written (June 1792.) This circumstance, apparently trivial, is very explanatory. To what end had *Clingman* the custody of this note all that time if it was not part of a project to lay the foundation for some false accusation?

It appears from No. V. that *Fraunces* had said, or was stated to have said, something to my prejudice. If my memory serves me aright, it was that he had been my agent in some speculations. When *Fraunces* was interrogated concerning it, he absolutely denied that he said any thing of the kind. The charge which this same *Fraunces* afterwards preferred against me to the House of Representatives, and the fate of it, have been already mentioned. It is illustrative of the nature of the combination which was formed against me.

There are other features in the documents which are relied upon to constitute the charge against me, that are of a nature to corroborate the inference to be drawn from the particulars which have been noticed. But there is no need to be over minute. I am much mistaken if the view which has been taken of the subject is not sufficient, without any thing further, to establish my innocence with every discerning and fair mind.

I proceed in the next place to offer a frank and plain solution of the enigma, by giving a history of the origin and progress of my connection with Mrs. Reynolds, of its discovery, real and pretended by the husband, and of the disagreeable embarrassments to which it exposed me. This history will be supported by the letters of Mr. and Mrs. Reynolds, which leave no room for doubt of the principal facts, and at the same time explain with precision the objects of the little notes from me which have been published, shewing clearly that such of them as have related to money had no reference to any concern in speculation. As the situation which will be disclosed, will fully explain every ambigious appearance, and meet satisfactorily the written documents, nothing more can be requisite to my justification. For frail indeed will be the tenure by which the most blameless man will hold his reputation, if the assertions of three of the most abandoned characters in the community, two of them stigmatized by the discrediting crime which has been mentioned, are sufficient to blast it—The business of accusation would soon become in such a case, a regular trade, and men's reputations would be bought and sold like any marketable commodity.

Some time in the summer of the year 1791 a woman called at my house in the city of Philadelphia and asked to speak with me in private. I attended her into a room apart from the family. With a seeming air of affliction she informed that she was a daughter of a Mr. Lewis, sister to a Mr. G. Livingston of the State of New-York, and wife to a Mr. Reynolds whose father was in the Commissary Department during the war with Great Britain, that her husband, who for a long time had treated her very cruelly, had lately left her, to live with another woman, and in so destitute a condition, that though desirous of returning to her friends she had not the means—that knowing I was a citizen of New-York, she had taken the liberty to apply to my humanity for assistance.

I replied, that her situation was a very interesting one—that I was disposed to afford her assistance to convey her to her friends, but this at the moment not being convenient to me (which was the fact) I must request the place of her residence, to which I should bring or send a small supply of money. She told me the street and the number of the house where she lodged. In the evening I put a bank-bill in my pocket and went to the house. I inquired for Mrs. Reynolds and was shewn up stairs, at the head of which she met me and conducted me into a bed room. I took the bill out of my pocket and gave it to her. Some conversation ensued from which it was quickly apparent that other than pecuniary consolation would be acceptable.

After this, I had frequent meetings with her, most of them at my own house; Mrs. Hamilton with her children being absent on a visit to her father. In the course of a short time, she mentioned to me that her husband had solicited a reconciliation, and affected to consult me about it. I advised to it, and was soon after informed by her that it had taken place. She told me besides that her husband had been engaged in speculation, and she believed could give information respecting the conduct of some persons in the department which would be useful. I sent for Reynolds who came to me accordingly.

In the course of our interview, he confessed that he had obtained a list of claims from a person in my department

which he had made use of in his speculations. I invited
him, by the expectation of my friendship and good
offices, to disclose the person. After some affectation of
scruple, he pretended to yield, and ascribed the infidelity
to Mr. Duer from whom he said he had obtained the list
in New-York, while he (Duer) was in the department.

As Mr. Duer had resigned his office some time before
the seat of government was removed to Philadelphia; this
discovery, if it had been true, was not very important—
yet it was the interest of my passions to appear to set
value upon it, and to continue the expectation of
friendship and good offices. Mr. Reynolds told me he
was going to Virginia, and on his return would point
out something in which I could serve him. I do not
know but he said something about employment in a
public office.

On his return he asked employment as a clerk in the
treasury department. The knowledge I had acquired of
him was decisive against such a request. I parried it by
telling him, what was true, that there was no vacancy in
my immediate office, and that the appointment of clerks
in the other branches of the department was left to the
chiefs of the respective branches. Reynolds alleged,
as *Clingman* relates No. IV (a) as a topic of complaint
against me that I had promised him *employment* and
had *disappointed* him. The situation with the wife would
naturally incline me to conciliate this man. It is possible

I may have used vague expressions which raised expectation; but the more I learned of the person, the more inadmissible his employment in a public office became. Some material reflections will occur here to a discerning mind. Could I have preferred my private gratification to the public interest, should I not have found the employment he desired for a man, whom it was so convenient to me, on my own statement, to lay under obligations. Had I had any such connection with him, as he has since pretended, is it likely that he would have wanted other employment? Or is it likely that wanting it, I should have hazarded his resentment by a persevering refusal? This little circumstance shews at once the delicacy of my conduct, in its public relations, and the impossibility of my having had the connection pretended with Reynolds.

The intercourse with Mrs. Reynolds, in the mean time continued; and, though various reflections, (in which a further knowledge of Reynold's character and the suspicion of some concert between the husband and wife bore a part) induced me to wish a cessation of it; yet her conduct, made it extremely difficult to disentangle myself. All the appearances of violent attachment, and of agonising distress at the idea of a relinquishment, were played with a most imposing art. This, though it did not make me entirely the dupe of the plot, yet kept me in a state of irresolution. My sensibility, perhaps my vanity, admitted the possibility of a real fondness; and led me to adopt the plan of a gradual discontinuance rather than of a sudden interruption, as least calculated to give pain, if a real partiality existed.

Mrs. Reynolds, on the other hand, employed every effort to keep up my attention and visits—Her pen was freely employed, and her letters were filled with those tender and pathetic effusions which would have been natural to a woman truly fond and neglected.

One day, I received a letter from her, which is in the appendix (No. I. b) intimating a discovery by her husband. It was matter of doubt with me whether there had been really a discovery by accident, or whether the time for the catastrophe of the plot was arrived.

The same day, being the 15th of December 1791, I received from Mr. Reynolds the letter (No. II. b) by which he informs me of the detection of his wife in the act of writing a letter to me, and that he had obtained from her a discovery of her connection with me, suggesting that it was the consequence of an undue advantage taken of her distress.

In answer to this I sent him a note, or message desiring him to call upon me at my office, which I think he did the same day.

He in substance repeated the topics contained in his letter and concluded as be bad done there, that he was resolved to have satisfaction.

I replied that he knew best what evidence he bad of the alleged connection between me and his wife, that I neither admitted nor denied it—that if he knew of any injury I had done him, intitling him to satisfaction, it lay with him to name it.

He travelled over the same ground as before, and again concluded with the same vague claim of satisfaction, but without specifying the kind, which would content him—It was easy to understand that be wanted money, and to prevent an explosion, I resolved to gratify him. But willing to manage his delicacy, if he had any, I reminded him that I had at our first interview made him a promise of service, that I was disposed to do it as far as might be proper, and in my power, and requested him to consider in what manner I could do it, and to write to me—He withdrew with a promise of compliance.

Two days after, the 17th of December, he wrote me the letter (No. III. b). The evident drift of this letter is to exaggerate the injury done by me, to make a display of sensibility and to magnify the attonement, which was to be required. It however comes to no conclusion, but proposes a meeting at the *George Tavern*, or at some other place more agreeable to me, which I should name.

On receipt of this letter, I called upon Reynolds, and assuming a decisive tone, told him, that I was tired of his indecision, and insisted upon his declaring to me explicitly what it was he aimed at—He again promised to explain by letter.

On the 19th, I received the promised letter (No. IV. b) the essence of which is that he was willing to take a thousand dollars as the plaister for his wounded honor.

I determined to give it to him, and did so in two payments, as per receipts (No. V and VI) dated the 22d of December and 3d of January. It is a little remarkable, that an avaricious speculating secretary of the treasury should have been so straitened for money as to be obliged to satisfy an engagement of this sort by two different payments!

On the 17th of January, I received the letter No. V. by which Reynolds invites me to *renew my visits to his wife.* He had before requested that I would see her no more. The motive to this step appears in the conclusion of the letter, *I rely* upon your befriending me, *if there should any thing offer that should be to my advantage,* as you *express a wish to befriend me.*" Is the pre-existence of a speculating connection reconcileable with this mode of expression?

If I recollect rightly, I did not immediately accept the invitation, nor 'till after I had received several very importunate letters from Mrs. Reynolds—See her letters No. VIH, (b) IX, X.

On the 24th of March following, I received a letter from *Reynolds,* No. XI, and on the same day one from his wife, No. XII. These letters will further illustrate the obliging co-operation of the husband with his wife to aliment and keep alive my connection with her.

The letters from Reynolds, No. XIII to XVI, are an additional comment upon the same plan. It was a persevering scheme to spare no pains to levy contributions upon my passions on the one hand, and upon my apprehensions of discovery on the other. It is probably to No. XIV that my note, in these words, was an answer: "To-morrow what is requested will be done. 'Twill hardly be possible *to-day*." The letter presses for the loan which is asked for *to-day*. A scarcity of cash, which was not very uncommon, is believed to have modelled the reply.

The letter No. XVII is a master-piece. The husband there forbids my future visits to his wife, chiefly because I was careful to avoid publicity. It was probably necessary to the project of some deeper treason against me that I should be seen at the house. Hence was it contrived, with all the caution on my part to avoid it, that *Clingman* should occasionally see me.

The interdiction was every way welcome, and was, I believe, strictly observed. On the second of June following, I received the letter No. XVIII, from Mrs. Reynolds, which proves that it was not her plan yet to let me off—It was probably the prelude to the letter from Reynolds, No. XIX, soliciting a *loan* of 300 dollars towards a subscription to the Lancaster Turnpike. *Clingman's* statement No. IV, admits, on the information of Reynolds, that to this letter the following note from me was an answer—"*It is utterly out of my power, I assure you 'pon my honour to comply with your request. Your note is returned.*" The letter itself demonstrates, that here was no concern in speculation on my part—that the money is asked as a *favour* and as a *loan*, to be reimbursed simply and without profit *in less than a fortnight*. My answer shews that even the loan was refused.

The letter No. XX, from *Reynolds*, explains the object of my note in these words, *"Inclosed are* 50 *dollars, they could not be sent sooner,"* proving that this sum, was also begged for in a very apologetic style as a mere loan.

The letters of the 24th and 30th of August, No. XXI and XXII, furnished the key to the affair of the 200 dollars mentioned by *Clingman* in No. IV, shewing that this sum was likewise asked by way of loan, towards furnishing a small boarding-house which *Reynolds* and his wife were or pretended to be about to set up.

These letters collectively, furnish a complete elucidation of the nature of my transactions with *Reynolds*. They resolve them into an amorous connection with his wife, detected, or pretended to be detected by the husband, imposing on me the necessity of a pecuniary composition with him, and leaving me afterwards under a duress for fear of disclosure, which, was the instrument of levying upon me from time to time *forced loans*—They apply directly to this state of things, the notes which *Reynolds* was so careful to preserve, and which had been employed to excite suspicion.

Four, and the principal of these notes have been not only generally but particularly explained—I shall briefly notice the remaining two.

"My dear Sir, I expected to have heard the day after I

had the pleasure of seeing you." This fragment, if truly a part of a letter to *Reynolds*, denotes nothing more than a disposition to be civil to a man, whom, as I said before, it was the interest of my passions to conciliate. But I verily believe it was not part of a letter to him, because I do not believe that I ever addressed him in such a stile—It may very well have been part of a letter to some other person, procured by means of which I am ignorant, or it may have been the beginning of an intended letter, torn off, thrown into the chimney in my office, which was a common practice, and there or after it had been swept out picked up by Reynolds or some coadjutor of his. There appears to have been more than one clerk in the department some how connected with him.

The endeavour shewn by the letter No. XVII, to induce me to render my visits to Mrs. Reynolds more public, and the great care with which my little notes were preserved, justify the belief that at a period, before it was attempted, the idea of implicating me in some accusation, with a view to the advantage of the accusers, was entertained. Hence the motive to pick up and preserve any fragment which might favour the idea of friendly or confidential correspondence.

2dly. "The person Mr. Reynolds inquired for on Friday waited for him all the evening at his house from a little after seven. Mr. R. may see him at any time to-day or to-morrow between the hours of two and three."

Mrs. Reynolds more than once communicated to me,

that Reynolds would occasionally relapse into discontent at his situation—would treat her very ill—hint at the assassination of me—and more openly threaten, by way of revenge, to inform Mrs. Hamilton—all this naturally gave some uneasiness. I could not be absolutely certain whether it was artifice or reality—In the workings of human inconsistency, it was very possible, that the same man might be corrupt enough to compound for his wife's chastity and yet have sensibility enough to be restless in the situation and to hate the cause of it.

Reflections like these induced me for some time to use palliatives with, the ill humours which were announced to me. Reynolds had called upon me in one of these discontented moods real or pretended. I was unwilling to provoke him by the appearance of neglect—and having failed to be at home at the hour he had been permitted to call, I wrote her the above note to obviate an ill impression.

The foregoing narrative and the remarks accompanying it have prepared the way for a perusal of the letters themselves. The more attention is used in this, the more entire will be the satisfaction which they will afford.

It has been seen that an explanation on the subject was had contemporarily that is in December 1792, with three members of Congress—F. A. Muhlenberg, J. Monroe, and A. Venable. It is proper that the circumstances of this transaction should be accurately understood.

The manner in which Mr. Muhlenberg became

engaged in the affair, is fully set forth in the document (No. I. a). It is not equally clear how the two other gentlemen came to embark in it. The phraseology, in reference to this point, in the close of (No. I.) and beginning of (No. II.) is rather equivocal. The gentlemen, if they please, can explain it.

But on the morning of the 15th of December 1792, the above mentioned gentlemen presented themselves at my office. Mr. Muhlenberg was then speaker. He introduced the subject by observing to me, that they *had discovered a very improper connection* between me and a Mr. Reynolds: extremely hurt by this mode of introduction, I arrested the progress of the discourse by giving way to very strong expressions of indignation. The gentlemen explained, telling me in substance that I had misapprehended them—that they did not take the fact for established—that their meaning was to apprise me that unsought by them, information had been given them of an improper pecuniary connection between Mr. Reynolds and myself; that they had thought it their duty to pursue it and had become possessed of some documents of a suspicious complexion—that they had contemplated laying the matter before the President, but before they did this they thought it right to apprise me of the affair and to afford an opportunity of explanation; declaring at the same time that their agency in the matter was influenced solely by a sense of public duty and by no motive of personal ill will. If my memory be correct, the notes from me in a disguised hand were now shewn to me which without a moment's hesitation I acknowledged to be mine.

I replied, that the affair was now put upon a different footing—that I always stood ready to meet fair inquiry with frank communication—that it happened, in the present instance, to be in my power by written documents to remove all doubts as to the real nature of the business, and fully to convince, that nothing of the kind imputed to me did in fact exist. The same evening at my house was by mutual consent appointed for an explanation.

I immediately after saw Mr. Wolcott, and for the first time informed him of the affair and of the interview just had; and delivering into his hands for perusal the documents of which I was possessed, I engaged him to be present at the intended explanation in the evening.

In the evening the proposed meeting took place, and Mr. Wolcott according to my request attended. The information, which had been received to that time, from *Clingman*, *Reynolds* and his wife, was communicated to me and the notes were I think again exhibited.

I stated in explanation, the circumstances of my affair with Mrs. Reynolds and the consequences of it and in confirmation produced the documents (No. I. b, to XXII.) One or more of the gentlemen (Mr. Wolcott's certificate No. XXIV, mentions one, Mr. Venable, but

I think the same may be said of Mr. Muhlenberg) was struck with so much conviction, before I had gotten through the communication that they delicately urged me to discontinue it as unnecessary. I insisted upon going through the whole and did so. The result was a full and unequivocal acknowledgment on the part of the three gentlemen of perfect satisfaction with the explanation and expressions of regret at the trouble and embarrassment which had been occasioned to me. Mr. Muhlenberg and Mr. Venable, in particular manifested a degree of sensibility on the occasion. Mr. Monroe was more cold but intirely explicit.

One of the gentlemen, I think, expressed a hope that I also was satisfied with their conduct in conducting the inquiry—I answered, that they knew I had been hurt at the opening of the affair—that this excepted, I was satisfied with their conduct and considered myself as having been treated with candor or with fairness and liberality, I do not now pretend to recollect the exact terms. I took the next morning a memorandum of the substance of what was said to me, which will be seen by a copy of it transmitted in a letter to each of the gentlemen No. XXV.

I deny absolutely, as alleged by the editor of the publication in question, that I intreated a suspension of the communication to the President, or that from the beginning to the end of the inquiry, I asked any favour or indulgence whatever, and that I discovered any symptom different from that of a proud consciousness of innocence.

Some days after the explanation I wrote to the three gentlemen the letter No. XXVI already published. That letter evinces the light in which I considered myself as standing in their view.

I received from Mr. Muhlenberg and Mr. Monroe in answer the letters No. XXVII and XXVIII.

Thus the affair remained 'till the pamphlets No. V and VI of the history of the U. States for 1796 appeared; with the exception of some dark whispers, which were communicated to me by a friend in Virginia, and to which I replied by a statement of what had passed.

When I saw No. V though it was evidence of a base infidelity somewhere, yet firmly believing that nothing more than a want of due care was chargeable upon either of the three gentlemen who had made the inquiry, I immediately wrote to each of them a letter of which No. XXV is a copy in full confidence that their answer would put the whole business at rest. I ventured to believe, from the appearances on their part at closing our former interview on the subject, that their answers would have been both cordial and explicit.

I acknowledge that I was astonished when I came to read in the pamphlet No. VI the conclusion of the document No. V, containing the equivocal phrase *"We left him under an impression our suspicions were removed,"* which seemed to imply that this had been a mere piece of management, and that the impression given me had not been reciprocal. The appearance of duplicity incensed me; but resolving to proceed with caution and moderation, I thought the first proper step was to inquire of the gentlemen whether the paper was genuine. A letter was written for this purpose the copy of which I have mislaid.

I afterwards received from Messrs. Muhlenberg and Venable the letters No. XXIX, XXX, and XXXI.

Receiving no answer from Mr. Monroe, and hearing of his arrival at New-York I called upon him. The issue of the interview was that an answer was to be given by him, in conjunction with Mr. Muhlenberg and Mr. Venable on his return to Philadelphia, he thinking that as the agency had been joint it was most proper the answer should be joint, and informing me that Mr. Venable had told him he would wait his return.

I came to Philadelphia accordingly to bring the affair to a close; but on my arrival I found Mr. Venable had left the city for Virginia.

Mr. Monroe reached Philadelphia according to his appointment. And the morning following wrote me 3 note No. XXXII. While this note was on its way my lodgings I was on my way to his—I had a conversation with him from which we separated with a repetition of the assurance in the note—In the course the interviews with Mr. Monroe, the *equivoque* in document No. V, (a) and the paper of January 2d, 93, under his signature were noticed.

I received the day following the letter No. XXXIII, which I returned the answer No. XXXIV,—accompanied with the letter No. XXXV, which was succeeded by the letters No. XXXVI— XXXVII— XXXVIII XXXIX—XL. In due time the sequel of the correspondence will appear.

Though extremely disagreeable to me, for very obvious reasons, I at length determined in order that no cloud whatever might be left on the affair, to publish the documents which had been communicated to Messrs. Monroe, Muhlenberg and Venable, all which will be seen in the appendix from No. I, (b) to No. III, inclusively.

The information from *Clingman* of the 2d January 1793, to which the signature of Mr. Monroe is annexed, seems to require an observation or two in addition to what is contained in my letter to him No. XXXIX.

Clingman first suggests that he had been apprized of my vindication through Mr. Wolcott a day or two after it had been communicated. It did not occur to me to inquire of Mr. Wolcott on this point, and he being now absent from Philadelphia, I cannot do it at this moment. Though I can have no doubt of the friendly intention of Mr. Wolcott, if the suggestion of Clingman in this particular be taken as true; yet from the condition of secrecy which was annexed to my communication, there is the strongest reason to conclude it is not true— If not true, there is besides but one of two solutions, either that he obtained the information from one of the three gentlemen who made the inquiry, which would have been a very dishonourable act in the party, or that he conjectured what my defence was from what he before knew it truly could be—For there is the highest probability, that through Reynolds and his wife, and as an accomplice, lie was privy to the whole affair. This last method of accounting for his knowledge would be conclusive on the sincerity and genuineness of the defence.

But the turn which *Clingman* gives to the matter must necessarily fall to the ground. It is, that Mrs. Reynolds denied her amorous connection with me, and represented the suggestion of it as a mere contrivance between *her husband* and *myself* to cover me, alleging that there had been a fabrication of letters and receipts to countenance it—The plain answer is that Mrs. Reynolds' own letters contradict absolutely this artful explanation of hers; if indeed she ever made it, of which *Clingman*'s assertion is no evidence whatever. These letters are proved by the affidavit No. XLI, though it will easily be conceived that the proof of them was rendered no easy matter by a lapse of near five years:—They shew explicitly the connection with her, the discovery of it by her husband and the pains she took to prolong it when I evidently wished to get rid of it—This cuts up, by the root, the pretence of a contrivance between the husband and myself to fabricate the evidences of it.

The variety of shapes which this woman could assume was endless. In a conversation between her and a gentleman whom I am not at liberty publicly to name, she made a voluntary confession of her belief and even knowledge, that I was innocent of all that had been laid to my charge by *Reynolds* or any other person of her acquaintance, spoke of me in exalted terms of esteem and respect, declared 'in the most solemn manner her extreme unhappiness lest I should suppose her accessory to the trouble which had been given me on that account, and expressed her fear that the resentment of Mr. Reynolds on *a particular score*, might have urged him to improper lengths of revenge—appearing at the same time extremely agitated and unhappy. With the gentleman who gives this information, I have never been in any relation personal or political that could be supposed to bias him—His name would evince that he is an impartial witness. And though I am not permitted to make a public use of it, I am permitted to refer any gentleman to the perusal of his letter in the hands of William Bingham, Esquire; who is also so obliging as to permit me to deposit with him for similar inspection all the original papers which are contained in the appendix to this narrative. The letter from the gentleman above alluded to has been already shewn to *Mr. Monroe*.

Let me now, in the last place recur to some comments, in which the hireling editor of the pamphlets No. V and VI has thought fit to indulge himself.

The first of them is that the *soft* language of one of my notes addressed to a man in the habit of threatening

me with disgrace, is incompatible with the idea of
innocence. The threats alluded to must be those of being
able to hang the Secretary of the Treasury. How does it
appear that Reynolds was in such a *habit*? No otherwise
than by the declaration of *Reynolds* and *Clingman*. If the
assertions of these men are to condemn me, there is
an end of the question. There is no need by elaborate
deductions from *parts* of their affections to endeavour
to establish what their assertions collectively affirm in
express terms—If they are worthy of credit I am guilty;
if they are not, all wiredrawn inferences from parts of
their story are mere artifice and nonsense. But no man,
not as debauched as themselves will believe them
independent of the positive disproof of their story in the
written documents.

As to the affair of threats (except those in Reynolds'
letters respecting the connection with his wife, which
it will be perceived were very gentle for the occasion)
not the least idea of the sort ever reached me 'till after
the imprisonment of Reynolds. Mr. Wolcott's certificate
shews my conduct in that case—notwithstanding the
powerful motives I may be presumed to have had to desire
the liberation of Reynolds, on account of my situation
with his wife, I cautioned Mr. Wolcott not to facilitate his
liberation, till the affair of the threat was satisfactorily
cleared up. The solemn denial of it in Reynolds' letter No.
XLII was considered by Mr. Wolcott as sufficient. This is

a further proof, that though in respect to my situation with his wife, I was somewhat in Reynolds's power, I was not disposed to make any improper concession to the apprehension of his resentment.

As to the threats intimated in his letters, the nature the cause will shew that the soft tone of my notes not only compatible with them, but a natural sequence of them.

But it is observed that the dread of the disclosure an amorous connection was not a sufficient cause my humility, and that I had nothing to lose as to reputation for chastity; concerning which the rid had fixed a previous opinion.

I shall not enter into the question what was the previous opinion entertained of me in this particular—nor how well founded, for it was indeed such as it is represented to have been. It is sufficient to say that there is a wide difference between vague rumours and suspicions and the evidence of a positive fact—no man not indelicately unprincipled, with the state of manners in this country, would be willing to have a conjugal infidelity fixed upon him with positive certainty—He would know that it would justly injure him with a considerable and respectable portion of the society—and especially no man, tender of the happiness of an excellent wife could without extreme pain look forward to the affliction which she might endure from the disclosure, especially a *public disclosure*, of the fact. Those best acquainted with the interior of my domestic life will best appreciate the force of such a consideration upon me.

The truth was, that in both relations and especially the last, I dreaded extremely a disclosure—and was willing to make large sacrifices to avoid it. It is true, that from the acquiescence of Reynolds, I had strong ties upon his secrecy, but how could I rely upon any tie upon so base a character. How could I know, but that from moment to moment he might, at the expence of his own disgrace, become the *mercenary* of a party, with whom to blast my character in *any way* is a favourite object!

Strong inferences are attempted to be drawn from the release of *Clingman* and *Reynolds* with the consent of the Treasury—from the want of communicativeness of Reynolds while in prison—from the subsequent disappearance of Reynolds and his wife, and from their not having been produced by me in order to be confronted at the time of the explanation.

As to the first, it was emphatically the transaction of Mr. Wolcott the then Comptroller of the Treasury, and was bottomed upon a very adequate motive—and one as appears from the document No. I, (a) early contemplated in this light by that officer. It was certainly of more consequence to the public to detect and expel from the bosom of the Treasury Department an unfaithful Clerk to prevent future and extensive mischief, than to disgrace and punish two worthless individuals. Besides that a powerful influence foreign to me was exerted to procure indulgence to them—that of Mr. Muhlenberg and Col. Burr—that of Col. Wadsworth, which though insidiously placed to my account was to the best of my recollection utterly unknown to me at the time, and according to the confession of Mrs. Reynolds herself, was put in motion by her entreaty. Candid men will derive strong evidence of my innocence and delicacy, from the reflection, that under circumstances so peculiar, the culprits were compelled to give a real and substantial equivalent for the relief which they obtained from a department, *over which I presided.*

The backwardness of Reynolds to enter into detail, while in jail, was an argument of nothing but that conscious of his inability to communicate any particulars which could be supported, he found it more convenient to deal in generals, and to keep up appearances by giving promises for the future.

As to the disappearance of the parties after the liberation, how am I answerable for it? Is it not presumable, that the instance discovered at the Treasury was not the only offence of the kind of which they were guilty? After one detection, is it not very probable that Reynolds fled to avoid detection in other cases? But exclusive of this, it is known and might easily be proved that Reynolds was considerably in debt! What more natural for him than to fly from his creditors after having been once exposed by confinement for such a crime? Moreover, atrocious as his conduct had been towards me, was it not natural for him to fear that my resentment might be excited at the discovery of it, and that it might have been deemed a sufficient reason for retracting the indulgence, which was shewn by withdrawing the prosecution and for recommencing it?

One or all of these considerations will explain the disappearance of Reynolds without imputing it to me as a method of getting rid of a dangerous witness.

That disappearance rendered it impracticable, if it had been desired to bring him forward to be confronted. As to *Clingman* it was not pretended that he knew any thing of what was charged upon me, otherwise than by the notes which he produced, and the information of Reynolds and his wife. As to Mrs. Reynolds, she in fact appears by *Clingman's* last story to have remained, and to have been accessible through him, by the gentleman who had undertaken the inquiry. If they supposed it necessary to the elucidation of the affair, why did not they bring her forward?

There can be no doubt of the sufficiency of Clingman's influence, for this purpose, when it is understood that Mrs. Reynolds and he afterwards lived together as man and wife. But to what purpose the confronting? What would it have availed to the elucidation of truth, if Reynolds and his wife had impudently made allegations which I denied. Relative character and the written documents must still determine. These could decide without it, and they were relied upon. But could it be expected, that I should so debase myself as to think it necessary to my vindication to be confronted with a person such as Reynolds? Could I have borne to suffer my veracity to be exposed to the humiliating competition?

For what?—why, it is said, to tear up the last twig of jealousy—but when I knew that I possessed written documents which were decisive, how could I foresee that any twig of jealousy would remain? When the proofs I did produce to the gentlemen were admitted by them to be completely satisfactory, and by some of them to be more than sufficient, how could I dream of the expediency of producing more—how could I imagine that every twig of jealousy was not plucked up?

If after the recent confessions of the gentlemen themselves, it could be useful to fortify the proof of the full conviction my explanation had wrought, I might appeal to the total silence concerning this charge, when at a subsequent period, in the year 1793, there was such an active legislative persecution of me. It might not even perhaps be difficult to establish, that it came under the eye of Mr. Giles, and that he discarded it as the plain case of a private amour unconnected with any thing that was the proper subject of a public attack.

Thus has my desire to destroy this slander, completely, led me to a more copious and particular examination of it, than I am sure was necessary. The bare perusal of the letters from Reynolds and his wife is sufficient to convince my greatest enemy that there is nothing worse in the affair than an irregular and indelicate amour. For this, I bow to the just censure which it merits. I have paid pretty severely for the folly and can never recollect it without disgust and self condemnation—It might seem affectation to say more.

To unfold more clearly the malicious intent, by which the present revival of the affair must have been influenced—I shall annex an affidavit of Mr. Webster tending to confirm my declaration of the utter falsehood of the assertion, that a menace of publishing the papers which have been published had arrested the progress of an attempt to hold me up as a candidate for the office of President. Does this editor imagine that lie will escape the just odium which awaits him by the miserable subterfuge of saying that he had the information from a respectable citizen of New-York? Till he names the author the inevitable inference must be that he has fabricated the tale.

APPENDIX

ALEXANDER HAMILTON.
Philadelphia, July, 1797.
No. I. (a)
Philadelphia, 13th *of December*, 1792.
Jacob Clingman being a clerk in my employment, and becoming involved in a prosecution commenced against James Reynolds, by the comptroller of the treasury, on a charge or information exhibited before Hillary Baker, Esq. one of the aldermen of this city, for subornation of perjury, whereby they had obtained money from the treasury of the United States, he (Clingman) applied to me for my aid and friendship on behalf of himself and Reynolds, to get them released or discharged from the prosecution. I promised, so far as respected Clingman, but not being particularly acquainted with Reynolds, in a great measure declined, so far as respected him. In company with Col. Burr, I waited on Col. Hamilton, for the purpose, and particularly recommended Clingman, who had hitherto sustained a good character. Col.

Hamilton signified a wish to do all that was consistent. Shortly after I waited on the comptroller, for the same purpose, who seemed to have some difficulties on the subject; and from some information I had, in the mean time, received, I could not undertake to recommend Reynolds; as I verily believed him to be a rascal; which words I made use of to the comptroller. On a second interview with the comptroller, on the same subject, the latter urged the propriety of Clingman's delivering up a certain list of money due to individuals, which Reynolds and Clingman were said to have in their possession, and of his informing him of whom, or thro' whom, the same was obtained from the public offices: on doing which, Clingman's request might, perhaps, be granted with greater propriety. This, Clingman, I am informed, complied with, and also refunded the money or certificates, which they had improperly obtained from the treasury. After which, I understand the action against both was withdrawn, and Reynolds discharged from imprisonment, without any further interference of mine whatsoever. During the time this business was thus depending, and which lasted upwards of three weeks, Clingman, unasked, frequently dropped hints to me, that Reynolds had it in his power, very materially to injure the secretary of the treasury, and that Reynolds knew several very improper transactions of his. I paid little or no attention to those hints, but when they were frequently repeated, and it was even added that Reynolds said, he had it in his power to hang the secretary of the treasury, that he was deeply concerned in speculation, that he had frequently advanced money to him (Reynolds) and other insinuations of an improper nature, it created considerable uneasiness on my mind, and I conceived it my duty to consult with some friends on the subject.—Mr. Monroe and Mr. Venable were informed of it yesterday morning.

Signed by Mr. Muhlenburg.

No. II. (a)
Philadelphia, 13th *December*, 1792.

Being informed yesterday in the morning, that a person of the name of Reynolds, from Virginia, Richmond, was confined in the jail, upon some criminal prosecution, relative to certificates, and that he had intimated, he could give some intelligence of speculations by Mr. Hamilton, which should be known, we immediately called on him, as well to be informed of the situation of the man, as of those other matters, in which the public might be interested. We found it was not the person, we had been taught to believe, but a man of that name from New-York, and who had, for some time past resided in this city.

Being there, however, we questioned him respecting the other particular: he informed us, that he could give information of the misconduct, in that respect, of a person high in office, but must decline it for the present, and until relieved, which was promised him, that evening: that at ten to-day, he would give us a detail of whatever he knew on the subject. He affirmed, he had a person in high office, in his power, and has had, a long time past: That he had written to him in terms so abusive, that no person should have submitted to it, but that he dared not to resent it. That Mr. Wolcott was in the same department and, he supposed, under his influence or controul.

And, in fact, expressed himself in such a manner, as to leave no doubt he meant Mr. Hamilton. That he expected to he relieved by Mr. Wolcott, at the instance of that person, although he believed that Mr. Wolcott, in instituting the prosecution, had no improper design. That he was satisfied the prosecution was set on foot, only to keep him low, and oppress him, and ultimately drive him away, in order to prevent his using the power he had over him;—that he had had, since his residence here, for eighteen months, many private meetings with that person, who had often promised to put him into employment, but had disappointed him:—That on hearing the prosecution was commenced against him, he applied to this person for counsel, who advised him to keep out of the way, for a few days:—That a merchant came to him, and offered, as a volunteer, to be his bail, who, he suspects, had been instigated by this person, and after being decoyed to the place, the merchant wished to carry him, he refused being his bail, unless he would deposit a sum of money to some considerable amount, which he could not do, and was, in consequence, committed to prison:—As well as we remember, he gave, as a reason why he could not communicate to us, what he knew of the facts alluded to, that he was apprehensive, it might prevent his discharge, but that he would certainly communicate the whole to us, at ten this morning; at which time, we were informed, he had absconded, or concealed himself.

Signed by James Monroe and
Abraham Venable.

No. III. (a)
Philadelphia, 13th December, 1792.
Being desirous, on account of their equivocal complection, to examine into the suggestions which had been made us respecting the motive for the confinement and proposed enlargement of James Reynolds, from the jail of this city, and inclined to suspect, for the same reason, that, unless it were immediately done, the opportunity would be lost, as we were taught to suspect he would leave the place, immediately after his discharge, we called at his house last night for that purpose; we found Mrs. Reynolds alone. It was with difficulty, we obtained from her, any information on

the subject, but at length she communicated to us the following particulars:

That since Col. Hamilton was secretary of the treasury, and at his request, she had burned a considerable number of letters from him to her husband, and in the absence of the latter, touching business between them, to prevent their being made public;—she also mentioned that Mr. Clingman had several anonymous notes addressed to her husband, which, she believed, were from Mr. Hamilton (which we have) with an endorsement "from secretary Hamilton, Esq." in Mr. Reynolds's hand writing:—That Mr. Hamilton offered her his assistance to go to her friends, which he advised:—That he also advised that her husband should leave the parts, not to be seen here again, and in which case, he would give something clever. That she was satisfied this wish for his departure did not proceed from friendship to him, but upon account of his threat, that he could tell something, that would make some of the heads of departments tremble. — That Mr. Wadsworth had been active in her behalf, first at her request; but, in her opinion, with the knowledge and communication of Mr. Hamilton, whose friend he professed to be; that he had been at her house yesterday and mentioned to her, that two gentlemen of Congress had been at the jail to confer with her husband; enquired if she knew what they went for; observed, he knew, Mr. Hamilton had enemies, who would try to prove some speculations on him, but, when enquired into, he would be found immaculate:—to which, she replied, she rather doubted it. We saw in her possession two notes; one in the name of Alexander Hamilton, of the sixth of December, and the other signed " S. W." purporting to have been written yesterday, both expressing a desire to relieve her.

She denied any recent communication with Mr. Hamilton, or that she had received any money from him lately.

Signed James Monroe and
F. A. Muhlenberg.

No. IV. (a)
Philadelphia, 13th December 1792.

Jacob Clingman has been engaged in some negociations with Mr. Reynolds, the person, who has lately-been discharged from a prosecution instituted against him by the comptroller of the treasury:—That his acquaintance commenced in September 1791:—That a mutual confidence and intimacy existed between them:—That in January or February last, he saw Col. Hamilton, at the house of Reynolds;—immediately on his going into the house Col. Hamilton left it;—That in a few days after, he (Clingman) was at Mr. Reynold's house, with Mrs. Reynolds, her husband being then out, some person knocked at the door; he arose and opened it, and saw that it was Col. Hamilton: Mrs. Reynolds went to the door; he delivered a paper to her, and that he was ordered to give Mr. Reynolds that: but asked Mrs. Reynolds, who could order the secretary of the treasury of the United States to give that; she replied, that she supposed he did not want to be known:—This happened in the night. He asked her how long Mr. Reynolds had been acquainted with Col. Hamilton; she replied some months;—That Col. Hamilton had assisted her husband; that some few days before that time, he had received upwards of eleven hundred dollars of Col. Hamilton. Some time after this, Clingman was at the house of Reynolds, and saw Col. Hamilton come in, he retired and left him there. A little after Duer's failure, Reynolds told Clingman in confidence, that if Duer had held up three days longer, he should have made fifteen hundred pounds, by the assistance of Col. Hamilton: that Col. Hamilton had informed him that he was connected with Duer. Mr. Reynolds also said, that Col. Hamilton had made thirty thousand dollars by speculation; that Col. Hamilton had supplied him with money to speculate. That, about June last, Reynolds told Clingman, that he had applied to Col. Hamilton, for money to subscribe to the turnpike road at Lancaster, and had received a note from him, in these words, "It is utterly out of my power, I assure you," upon my honor, to comply with your request. Your "note is returned." Which original note, accompanying this, has been in Clingman's possession ever since.

Mr. Reynolds has once or twice mentioned to Clingman, that he had it in his power to hang Col. Hamilton; that if he wanted money he was obliged to let him have it:—That he (Clingman) has occasionally lent money to Reynolds, who always told him, that he could always get it from Col. Hamilton, to repay it.—That on one occasion Clingman lent him two hundred dollars, that Reynolds promised to pay him thro' the means of Col. Hamilton, that he went with him, saw him go into Col. Hamilton's;—that after he came out, he paid him one hundred dollars, which, he said, was part of the sum he had got; and paid the balance in a few days; the latter sum paid was said to have been from Col. Hamilton, after his return from Jersey, having made a visit to the manufacturing society there. After a warrant was issued against Reynolds, upon a late prosecution, which was instituted against him, Clingman seeing Reynolds, asked him why he did not apply to his friend Col. Hamilton, he said he would go immediately, and went accordingly;— he said afterwards, that Col. Hamilton advised him to keep out of the way, a few days, and the matter would be settled.

That after this time, Henry Seckel went to Reynolds, and offered to be his bail, if he would go with him to Mr. Baker's office, where he had left the officer, who had the warrant in writing;—that he prevailed on Reynolds to go with him;— that after Reynolds was taken into custody, Seckel refused to become his bail, unless he would deposit, in his possession, property to the value of four hundred pounds; upon which, Reynolds wrote to Col. Hamilton, and Mr. Seckel carried the note;—after two or three times going, he saw Col. Hamilton; Col. Hamilton said, he knew Reynolds and his father;—that his father was a good whig in the late war; that was all he could say: That it was not in his power to assist him; in consequence of which, Seckel refused to be his bail, and Reynolds was imprisoned. Mr. Reynolds also applied to a Mr. Francis, who is one of the clerks in the treasury department: he said he could not do anything, without the consent of Mr. Hamilton; that he would apply to him. He applied to Mr. Hamilton; who told him, that it would not be prudent; if he did, he must leave the department.

After Reynolds was confined, Clingman asked Mrs. Reynolds, why she did not apply to Col. Hamilton, to dismiss him, as the money was ready to be refunded, that had been received;—she replied, that she had applied to him, and he had sent her to Mr. Wolcott, but directed her not to let Mr. Wolcott know, that he had sent her there; notwithstanding this injunction she did let Mr. Wolcott know, by whom she had been sent; who appeared tobe surprised at the information, but said, he would do what he could for her, and would consult Col. Hamilton on the occasion. Col. Hamilton advised her to get some person of respectability to intercede for her husband, and mentioned Mr. Muhlenburg.

Reynolds continued to be kept in custody, for some

time; during which time, Clingman had conversation with Mr. Wolcott, who said, if he would give up a list of claims which he had, he should be released:—After this, Mrs. Reynolds informed Clingman, that Col. Hamilton had told her, that Clingman should write a letter to Mr. Wolcott, and a duplicate of the same to himself, promising to give up the list, and refund the money, which had been obtained on a certificate, which had been said to have been improperly obtained.

Clingman asked Mrs. Reynolds for the letters, that her husband had received from Col. Hamilton, from time to time, as he might probably use them to obtain her husband's liberty;—she replied, that Col. Hamilton had requested her to burn all the letters, that were in his hand writing, or that had his name to them: which she had done; he pressed her to examine again, as she might not have destroyed the whole, and they would be useful;—She examined and found notes, which are herewith submitted, and which, she said, were notes from Col. Hamilton.

Mrs. Reynolds told Clingman, that having heard, that her husband's father was, in the late war, a commissary under the direction of Col. Wadsworth, waited on him, to get him to intercede for her husband's discharge:—he told her, he would give her his assistance, and said, now you have made me your friend, you must apply to no person else.—That on Sunday evening Clingman went to the house of Reynolds, and found Col. Wadsworth there: he was introduced to Col. Wadsworth by Mrs. Reynolds: Col Wadsworth told him, lie had seen Mr. Wolcott;—that Mr. Wolcott would do any thing for him (Clingman) and Reynolds's family, that he could;—that he had called on Col. Hamilton but had not seen him;— but he might tell Mr. Muhlenburg, that a friend of his (Clingman's) had told him, that Col. Wadsworth was a countryman and schoolmate of Mr. Ingersoll, and that Col. Wadsworth was also intimate with the governor, and that the governor would do almost any thing to oblige him;—that his name must not be mentioned to Mr. Muhlenburg, as telling him this; but that if Mr. Muhlenburg could be brought to speak to him first, on the subject, he would then do any thing in his power for them; and told him not to speak to him, if he should meet him in the street, and said, if his name was mentioned, that he would do nothing:—That on Wednesday, Clingman saw Col. Wadsworth at Reynolds's house; he did not find her at home, but left a note; but on going out he met her, and said he had seen every body, and done every thing.

Mrs. Reynolds told Clingman, that she had received money of Col. Hamilton, since her husband's confinement, enclosed in a note, which note she had burned.

After Reynolds was discharged, which was eight or nine o'clock on Wednesday evening:—about twelve o'clock at night, Mr. Reynolds sent a letter to Col. Hamilton by a girl; which letter Clingman saw delivered to the girl; Reynolds followed the girl, and Clingman followed him;—he saw the girl go into Col. Hamilton's house;—Clingman then joined Reynolds, and they walked back and forward in the street, until the girl returned, and informed Reynolds, that he need not go out of town that night, but call on him, early in the morning. In the morning, between seven and eight o'clock, he saw Reynolds go to Col. Hamilton's house and go in: he has not seen him since, and supposes he has gone out of the state.

Mr. Clingman further adds, that some time ago, he was informed by Mr. and Mrs. Reynolds, that he had books containing the amount of the cash due to the Virginia line, at his own house at New-York, with liberty to copy, and was obtained thro' Mr. Duer.

The above contains the truth to the best of my knowledge and recollection, and to which I am ready to make oath.

Given under my hand, this 13th of December, 1792.

Signed by Jacob Clingman.

No. I.

Col. Hamilton

Dear Sir

I have not tim to tell you the cause of my present

troubles only that Mr. has rote you this morning and I know not wether you have got the letter or not and he has swore that If you do not answer It or If he dose not se or hear from you to day he will write Mrs. Hamilton he has just Gone oute and I am a Lone I think you had better come here one moment that you May know the Cause then you will the better know how to act Oh my God I feel more for you than myself and wish I had never been born to give you so much unhappiness do not write to him no not a Line but come here soon do not send or leave any thing in his power

Maria

No. II.

Philadelphia, 15th December, 1791.

Sir

I am very sorry to find out that I have been so Cruelly treated by a person that I took to be my best friend instead of that my greatest Enimy. You have deprived me of every thing thats near and dear to me, I discovred whenever I Came into the house, after being out I found Mrs. Reynolds weeping I ask'd her the Cause of being so unhappy. She always told me that she had bin Reding, and she could not help Crying when she Red any thing that was Afecting. but seing her Repeatedly in that Setevation gave me some suspicion to think that was not the Cause, as fortain would have it. before matters was carred to two great a length. I discovered a letter directed to you which I copied of and put it in the place where I found it without being discovered by Her. and then the evening after. I was Curious anough to watch her. and see give a leter to a Black man in Market Street, which I followed him to your door, after that I Returned home some time in the evening, and I broached the matter to her and Red the Copy to her which she fell upon her knees and asked forgiveness and discovered every thing to me Respecting the matter and ses that she was unhappy, and not knowing what to do without some assistance. She Called on you for the lone of some money, which you toald her you would call on her the Next Evening, which accordingly you did. and there Sir you took the advantage a poor Broken harted woman, instead of being a Friend, you have acted the part of the most Cruelist man in existance. you have made a whole family miserable. She ses there is no other man that she Care for in this world, now Sir you have bin the Cause of Cooling her affections for me. She was a woman. I should as soon sespect an angiel from heven. and one where all my happiness was depending, and I would Sacrefise almost my life to make her Happy, but now I am determined to have satisfation. it shant be onely one mamily thats miserable, for I am Robbed of all happiness in this world I am determined to leve her. and take my daughter with me that Shant see her poor mother Lot. now Sir if I Cant see you at your house call and see me. for there is no person that Knowes any thing as yet. And I am tiremd to see you, by some means or other, for you have made me an unhappy man for eve. put it to your own case and Reflect one moment, that you should know shush a thing of your wife, would not you have satisfacton yes. and so will I before one day passes me more.

I am yours
James Reynolds.
Mr. Alexander Hamilton.

No. III.
Saturday Evening 17th *December,* 1791.
Sir,

I now have taken till tuesday morning to Consider on What Steps will be Best for me to take. I should not have let the matter Rested till then, if it had not been for the news of the death of my Sister, which it Semes as if all my troubles are Comming on me in one moment, if it had been any other person except yourself, that treated me as you have done. I should not have taken the trouble to Call on them more than once, *but your being in the Station of life* you are. induses me to way every Surcomcance well Respecting the matter it will be impossible for me ever to think of liveing or Reconsiling myself to Stay with a woman that I no has plased her affections on you. and you know if you Reflect one moment, that you have been the sole Cause of it. I have all Reason in the world to believe its true. I am that man that will always have Satisfaction by some means or other when treated ill. Especially when I am treated in the manner, as you have done, you may rest ashured that the matter as yet is Not known. If think proper to Call at the sign of the George tuesday morning at 8 oclock I will be there, for your house or office is no place to converse about these matters, if that is not agreeable to you. let me know what place I shall see you at. at that time, for I am determined to know what corse I shall take, more miserable I cant be than I am at present. let the consequence be as it will, for when I come into the house. I find the wife always weeping and praying that I wont leve her. And its all on your account, for if you had not seeked for her Ruin it would not have happined. Could you not have Relieved the disstressed without, transgressing in the mannor you have done. Sertainly you did not show the man of honnor. in taking the advantage of the afflicted, when Calling on you as a father and protector in the time of disstress. put that home to yourself and tell me what you would do in such a Case, or what amend Could be made to you or wether it would be possible to make any. you will answer no. it be impossible after being Robbed of all your happiness and your whole family made misseable. I know you are a man thats not void of feeling. I am not a man that wishes to do any thing Rashly, or plunge myself into Ruin, now if you think proper to se me at the place I have mentioned, or any other, please to let me no before, for I wish to be by ourselfs where we Can converse together, for if you do not Call on me or let me no where I Can see. you at that time. I shant call on yon after this.

I am yours
James Reynolds
Mr. Alexander Hamilton.

No. IV.
Philadelphia, 19th December, 1791.
Sir.
When we were last togeather you then would wis to know my Determination what I would do and. you exspess a wish to do any thing that was in your power to Serve me, its true its in your power to do a great deal for me, but its out of your power to do any thing that will Restore to me my Happiness again for if you should give me all you possess would not do it. god knowes I love the woman and wish every blessing may attend her, you have bin the Cause of Winning her love, and I Dont think I Can be Reconciled to live with Her, when I know I hant her love, now Sir I have Considered on the matter Serously. I have This preposial to make to you. give me the Sum Of thousand dollars and I will leve the town and take my daughter with me and go where my

Friend Shant here from me and leve her to Yourself to do for her as you thing proper. I hope you wont think my request is in a view of making Me Satisfaction for the injury done me. for there is nothing that you Can do will Compensate for it. your answer I shall expect This evening or in the morning early, as I am Determined to wate no longer till. I know my lot

yours
James Reynolds
Mr. Alexr. Hamilton

No. V.
Received December 22 of Alexander Hamilton six hundred dollars on account of a sum of one thousand dollars due to me.

James Reynolds

No. VI.
Received Philadelphia January 3. 1792 of Alexander Hamilton four hundred dollars in full of all demands

James Reynolds

No. VII.
Philadelphia 17th, January 1792.
Sir
I Suppose you will be surprised in my writing to you

Repeatedly as I do. But dont be Alarmed for its Mrs. R. wish to See you. and for My own happiness and hers. I have not the Least Objections to your Calling, as a friend to Boath of us. and must rely intirely on your and her honnor. when I conversed with you last. I told you it would be disagreeable to me for you to Call, but Sence, I am pritty well Convinsed, She would onely wish to See you as a friend, and sence I am Reconciled to live with her, I would wish to do every thing for her happiness and my own, and Time may ware of every thing. So dont fail in Calling as Soon as you Can make it Conveanant. and I Rely on your befriending me if there should anything Offer that would be to my advantage, as you Express a wish to befriend me. So I am

  yours to Serve
  James Reynolds
  Mr. Alexr. Hamilton.

No. VIII.
Monday Night, Eight C, L
Sir,

I need not acquaint that I had Ben Sick all moast Ever sence I saw you as I am sure you allready no It Nor would I solicit a favor wich Is so hard to obtain were It not for the Last time Yes Sir Rest assurred I will never ask you to Call on me again I have kept my Bed those tow dayes and now rise from My pilliow wich your Neglect has filled with the shorpest thorns I no Longer doubt what I have Dreaded to no but stop I do not wish to se you to to say any thing about my Late disappointment No I only do it to Ease a heart wich is ready Burst with Greef I can neither Eat or sleep I have Been on the point of doing the moast horrid acts at I shudder to think where I might been what will Become of me. In vain I try to Call reason to aid me but alas ther Is no Comfort for me I feel as If I should not Contennue long and all the wish I have Is to se you once more that I may my doubts Cleared up for God sake be not so voed of all humannity as to deni me this Last request but if you will not Call some time this night I no its late but any tim between this and twelve A Clock I shall be up Let me Intreat you If you wont Come to send me a Line oh my head I can rite no more do something to Ease My heart or Els I no not what I shall do for so I cannot live Commit this to the care of my maid be not offended I beg.

No. IX.
Wednesday Morning ten of Clock.
Dear Sir

I have kept my bed those tow days past but find my self mutch better at presant though yet full distreesed and shall till I se you fretting was the Cause of my Illness I thought you had been told to stay away from our house and yesterday with tears I my Eyes I beged Mr. once more to permit your visits and he told upon his honnour that he had not said anything to you and that It was your own fault believe me I scarce knew how to beleeve my senses and if my seturation was insuportable before I heard this It was now more so fear prevents my saing more only that I shal be misarable till I se you and if my dear freend has the Least Esteeme for the unhappy Maria whos greateest fault Is Loveing him he will come as soon as he shall get this and till that time My breast will be the seate of pain and woe.

adieu.

Col. Hamilton

P. S. If you cannot come this Evening to stay just come only for one moment as I shal be Lone Mr. is going to sup with a friend from New-York.

No. X.

Monday Morning.

the Girl tells me that you said If I wanted any thing that I should write this morning alas my friend want what what can ask for but peace wich you alone can restore to my tortured bosom and do My dear Col hamilton on my kneese Let me Intreatee you to reade my Letter and Comply with my request tell the bearer of this or give her a line you need not be the least affraid let me not die with fear have pity on me my freend for I deserve it I would not solicit this favor but I am sure It cannot injure you and will be all the happiness I Ever Expect to have But oh I am disstressed more than I can tell My heart Is ready to burst and my tears wich once could flow with Ease are now denied me Could I only weep I would thank heaven and bless the hand that

No. XI.
Sunday Evening 24th March. 1792.
Sir

On my entering the Room the last evening. I found Mrs Reynolds in a setuvation little different from distraction and for some time could not prevail on her to tell me the Cause, at last She informed me that you had been here likewise of a letter she had wrote you in a fright, which she need not have don as I Never intended doing any thing I told her but did it to humble Her. for the imprudent language she made yuse of to me. and You may Rest ashured sir, that I have not a wish to do any thing that may give you or your family a moments pain I know not what you may think of me. but suppose yourself for a moment in my setuvation, that your wife whom you tenderly love. should plase her affections on another object and hear her say. that all her happiness depends intirely on that object, what would you do in such a Case, would you have acted as I have don. I have Consented to things which I thought I never could have don. hut I have dun it to make life tolerable, and for the sake of a person whose happiness is dearer to me than my own. I have another afliction added to the Rest that IS almost insupportable. I find when ever you have been with her. she is Cheerful and kind, but when you have not in some time she is Quite to Reverse, and wishes to be alone by her self, but when I tell her of it. all her answer is she Cant help it. and hopes I will forgive her. shurely you Cannot wonder if I should act ever so imprudent, though at present if I could take all her Grief upon myself I would do it with pleashure. the excess of which alarm me untill now. I have had no idea of. I have spent this day at her bed side in trying to give her the Consolation which I myself stand in need of. she also tell me, you wish to see me tomorrow evening and then I shall Convince you. that I would not wish to trifle with you And would much Rather add to the happiness of all than to disstress any

am sir Your
James Reynolds
Mr. Alexr. Hamilton

No. XII.
Read this all
Sunday Night, one O Clock
My dear friend
In a state of mind which know language can paint I take up the pen but alas I know not what I write or

how to give you an idea of the anguish wich at this moment rends my heart yes my friend I am doomed to drink the bitter cup of affliction Pure and unmixed but why should I repine why pour forth my wretched soul in fruitless complainings for you have said It you have commanded and I must submit heaven tow Inexorable heaven Is deaf to my anguish and has marked me out for the child of sorrow oh my dear friend wether shall I fly for consolation oh all all consolation is shut against me there is not the least gleme of hope but oil merciful God forgive me and you my friend Comply with this Last Bequest Let me once more se you and unbosom Myself to you perhaps I shal be happier after It I have mutch to tell wich I dare not write And which you ought to know oh my dear Sir give me your advice for once In an Affair on wich depends my Existence Itself Think not my friend that I say this to make you come and se me and that I have nothing to tell you for heaven by which I declare knows that I have woes to relate wich I never Expected to have known accept by the name Come therefore to-morrow sometime or Els in the Evening do I beg you to come gracious God had I the world I would lay It at your feet If I could only se you oh I must or I shall lose my senses and It is not because I think to prevail on you to visit me again no my dear Col Hamilton I do not think of It but will when I se you do just as you tell me so doant be offended with me for pleadeing so hard to se you If you do not think it proper to come here Let me know by a line where I shal se you and what hour you need not put your name to It or mine Either Just direct Mr or Els leve It blank adieu my Ever dear Col hamilton you may form to yourself an Idea of my distress for I Cant desscribe It to you Pray for me and be kind to me Let me se you death now would be welcome Give

No. XIII.

Philadelphia 3d, April, 1792.

Sir

I hope you will pardon me in taking the liberty I do In troubling you so offen. it hurts me to let you Know my Setivation. I should take it as a protickeler if you would Oblige me with the lone of about thirty Dollars I am in hopes in a fue days I shall be In a more better Setivation. and then I shall Be able to make you ample Satisfaction for your Favours shewn me. I want it for some little Necssaries of life for my family, sir you granting the above favour this morning will very much Oblige your most Obedient and humble Servant

James Reynolds

Alex. Hamilton Esqr.

N B the inclose is a Receipt for Ninety dollars, that is if you Can Oblige me with the thirty, thats Including Boath Sums

Received Philadelphia 3d. April. 1792 of Alexander Hamilton Esqr. Ninety dollars which I promise to pay

on demand
  James Reynolds
  90, Dollars

No. XIV.

Philadelphia, 7th, April. 1792.
  Sir
I am sorry to inform you my setivation is as such. I am indebted to a man in this town about 45. dollars which he will wate no longer on me. now sir I am Sorrey to be troubleing you So Offen. which if you Can Oblige me with this *to day*. you will do me infenate service, that will pay Nearly all I owe in this town except yourself. I have some property on the North River wich I have Wrote to my Brother sell which as soon as it Come in my hands. I pay you every shilling with strictest Justice you Oblige me with, the inclose is the Receipt, for the amount I am sir with due Regard, your humble servant
  James Reynolds
  Alexr. Hamilton Esqr.
  Received Philadelphia. 7th. April. 1792. of Alexander Hamilton Esqr. Forty five dollars which I promise to pay on demand
  James Reynolds
  45 dollars

No. XV

Philadelphia, 17th. *April*. 1792.

Sir

I am sorry to be the barer of So disagreeable, an unhappy infermation. I must tell you Sir that I have bin the most unhappiest man. for this five days in Existance, Which you aught to be the last person I ever Should tell my troubls to. ever Sence the night you Calld and gave her the Blank Paper. She has treated me more Cruel than pen cant paint out. and Ses that She is determed never to be a wife to me any more, and Ses that it Is a plan of ours, what has past god knows I Freely forgive you and dont wish to give you fear or pain a moment on the account of it. now Sir I hope you will give me your advise as freely as if Nothing had eve passed Between us I think it is in your power to make matter all Easy again, and I suppose you to be that Man of fealling that you would wish to make every person happy Where it in you power I shall wate to See you at the Office if its Convenant. I am sir with Asteem yours

James Reynolds

Alexr Hamilton Esqr.

No. XVI.

Philadelphia, 23d. April. 1792.

Sir

I am sorry I am in this disagreeable sutivation which Obliges me to trouble you So offen as I do. but I hope it wont be long before it will be In my power to discharge what I am indebted to you Nothing will give me greater pleasure I must Sir ask the loan of thirty dollars more from you, which I shall esteem as a particular favour, and you may Rest ashured that I will pay you with Strickest Justice, for the Reliefe you have aforded me, the Inclosed is the Receipt for the thirty dollars. I shall wate at your Office. Sir for an answer I am sir your very Humble Servant

James Reynolds.

Alexr. Hamilton Esqr.

No. XVII.

Philadelphia, 2d May, 1792.

Sir

I must now for ever forbid you of visiting Mrs. R any more I was in hopes that it would in time ware off, but I find there is no hopes. So I determed to put a finell end to it. if it sin my power, for I find by your Seeing her onely Renews the Friendship, and likewise when you Call you are fearful any person Should See you am I a person of Such a bad Carector. that you would not wish to be seen in Coming in my house in the front way. all any Person Can say of me is that I am poore and I dont know if that is any Crime. So I must meet my fate. I have my Reasons for it for I cannot be Reconsiled to it. for there is know person Can tell the pain it gives me except the were plased in my sutivation I am sure the world would despise me if the Onely new what I have bin Reconsiled to, I am in hopes in a short time to make you amends for your favour Renderedm e

I am Sir your humble Servant.

J. Reynolds

Alexr. Hamilton Esqr.

No. XVIII.

Saturday Morning the June 2

Dear Sir

I once take up the pen to solicit The favor of seing again oh Col hamilton what have I done that you should thus Neglect me Is it because I am unhappy But stop I will not say you have for perhaps you have caled and have found no opportunity to Come In at least I hope you have I am now A lone and shall be for a few days I believe till Wensday though am not sartain and would wish to se you this Evening I poseble If not as soon as you can make It Convenent oh my deer freend how shal I plede Enough what shal I say Let me beg of you to Come and If you never se me again oh if you think It best I will submit to It and take a long and last adieu Mari

Col hamilton

for heaven sake keep me not In suspince Let me know your Intention Either by a Line or Catline.

No. XIX.

Sir

I am now under the necessity of asking a favour from you Which if Can Oblige me with the loan of three Hundred dollars, it will be in my power to make five hundred Before the Next week is out. and if you Can oblege me with it. you may rely on haveing of it again the last of Next Week, if I am alive and well, the use I wont it for is to Subscribe to the turn pike Road, there is a number of gentleman in town wants me to go up to Lancaster to Subscribe for them, no sir if you Can oblige as I want to leve town tomorrow morning and the books will be open for subscribing on monday morning Next, so that I shall have Little time to get there, you never Sir Can oblige me more than Complying with the above, please to let me know between this and 4 oClock if you dont I shant be able to go—from your Humble Sevt.

James Reynolds.

Alexr. Hamilton Esqr.

No. XX.

Philadelphia 23d June. 1792.

Honnored Sir,

Your Goodness will I hope overlook the present application you will infenately Oblige me if you Can let me have the Loan of fifty dollars, for a few days, what little money I had I put into the turnpike Scrip, and I dont like to sell At the low advance the are selling at. at present, as its very low. if you Can Oblige me with that much in the morning sir you shall have it in a short time again and you Will very much Oblige your Humble and Obed. Serv.

J. R

Alexr. Hamilton. Esq.

NB. you will I hope pardon me in taking the liberty to call to day. but my Necessaty is such that it Oblige me to do it: Sunday evening.

Received Philadelphia 24th June. 1792 of Alexander Hamilton Esq. Fifty Dollars, which I promise to pay on demand to the said Alexr. Hamilton or Order as witness my hand James Reynolds

50 Dollars

No. XXI.

Philadelphia 24th. August. 1792.

Honored Sir.

When I Conversed with you last I mentioned that I was going to moove. Sence that I have mooved I have taken a very convenant house for a boarding house, but being disappointed in receiving Some money, put it intirely out of my power to furnish the house I have taken. I have four genteal boarders will come to live with me, as soon as I Can get the Rooms furnished, dear Sir, this is my Setuvation. I am in no way of business, the Cash last lent me. inable me to pay my Rent, and some little debts I had Contracted for my Familys youse. now sir if I Can ask a favour once more of the loan of two Hundred dollars. I will give you Surity of all I process, for the payment of what I owe you. without your assistance, this time I dont know what I shall do. Mrs. Reynolds and myself has made a Calculation, and find with that much money will inable us to take in four boarders, and I am in hopes in the mean time will, something will turn up in my favour, which will enable me to keep myself and famy. dear Sir your Complying with the above will for ever, lay me under the greitist Obligation to you and I will, you may Rest ashured. Repay it again as soon as it is in my power.

I am Honored Sir with
Respect your most Obedt.
and Humble Servt.
James Reynolds
Vine Street No. 161 Second door
from the Corner of fifth Street
Alexr. Hamilton Esqr.

No. XXII.
Philadelphia 30th Aug. 1792.
Honored Sir,

you will I hope pardon me if I intrude on your goodness thinking the multiplycity of business, you have to encounter With, has been the cause of my not hereing from you. which induces me to write the Second time, flatering myself it will be in your Power to Comply with my Request, which I shall make it my whole Study, to Remit it to you as soon as its in my power your Compyance dear Sir will very much

Oblige your most
Obed. and Humble Servant.
James Reynolds
Vine street No. 161, one door from
the Corner of Fifth Street.
Alexander Hamilton, Esq.

No. XXIII.

City of Pennsylvania, ss.

Henry Seckel of the City aforesaid Merchant maketh oath that on or about the thirteenth day of November in the year one thousand seven hundred and ninety two Jacob Clingman sent for this Deponent to the house of Hilary Baker, Esquire, then Alderman, that this Deponent went accordingly to the house of the said Alderman and was there requested by the said Jacob Clingman to become his bail which he did upon the promise of the said Clingman to deposit with him a sum in certificates sufficient to cover and secure him for so becoming bail—That the said Clingman having failed to make the said deposit according to his promise this Deponent applied to the said Hilary Baker and obtained for him a warrant upon which the said Clingman was arrested and carried again to the said Hilary Baker—That said Clingman again urged this Deponent to become his bail but he declining said Clingman requested this Deponent to go and bring to him one James Reynolds from whom as this Deponent understood the said Clingman expected to obtain assistance towards his release from Custody—That this Deponent went accordingly to the said James Reynolds and in the name of Clingman engaged him to accompany the Deponent to the House of the said Alderman where the said

James Reynolds was also apprehended and detained That thereupon the said James Reynolds requested this Deponent to carry a letter for him to Alexander Hamilton then Secretary of the Treasury—that this Deponent carried the said letter as requested and after two or three calls found the said Alexander Hamilton and delivered the letter to him—that the said Hamilton after reading it mentioned to this Deponent that he had known the father of the said Reynolds during the war with Great-Britain, and would be willing to serve the said James, if he could with propriety, but that it was not consistent with the duty of his office to do what Reynolds now requested; and also mentioned to this Deponent that Reynolds and Clingman had been doing something very bad and advised this Deponent to have nothing to do with them lest he might bring himself into trouble—And this Deponent further saith that he never had any conversation or communication whatever with the said Alexander Hamilton respecting the said Reynolds or Clingman till the time of carrying the said letter. And this Deponent further saith that the said Clingman formerly lived with this Deponent and kept his books which as he supposes was the reason of his sending for this Deponent to become his bail thinking that this Deponent might be willing to befriend him.

HENRY SECKEL.

Sworn this 19th day of July
MDCCXCVII before me
Hilary Baker, Mayor.

No. XXIV.

Having perused the fifth and fixth numbers of a late publication in this City entitled "The History of the United States for the year 1796" and having reviewed certain letters and documents which have remained in my possession since the year 1792, I do hereby at the request of Alexander Hamilton Esquire

of New York Certify and declare,

That in the Month of December 1792, I was desired by Mr. Hamilton to be present at his house as the witness of an interview which had been agreed upon between himself and James Monroe, Frederick Augustus Muhlenberg and Abraham Venable, Esquires, with which I accordingly complied.

The object of the interview was to remove from the minds of those Gentleman, certain suspicions which had been excited by suggestions of James Reynolds then in Prison and Jacob Clingman a Clerk to Mr. Muhlenberg, (against both of whom prosecutions had been instituted for frauds against the United States,) that Mr. Hamilton had been concerned in promoting or assisting speculation in the public funds, contrary to Law and his duty as Secretary of the Treasury.

The conference was commenced on the part of Mr. Monroe by reading certain Notes from Mr. Hamilton and a Narrative of conversations which had been held with the said Reynolds and Clingman—After the grounds upon which the suspicions rested, had been fully stated, Mr. Hamilton entered into an explanation and by a variety of written documents, which were read, fully evinced, that there was nothing in the transactions to which Reynolds and Clingman had referred, which had any connection with, or relation to speculations in the Funds, claims upon the United States, or any public or official transactions or duties whatever. This was rendered so completely evident, that Mr. Venable requested Mr. Hamilton to desist from exhibiting further proofs. As however an explanation had been desired by the Gentleman before named, Mr. Hamilton insisted upon being allowed to read such documents as he possessed, for the purpose of obviating every shadow of doubt respecting the propriety of his Official conduct.

After Mr. Hamilton's explanation terminated Messrs. Monroe, Muhlenberg and Venable, severally acknowledged their entire satisfaction, that the affair had no relation to Official duties, and that it ought not to affect or impair the public confidence in Mr. Hamilton's character;—at the same time, they expressed their regrets at the trouble which the explanation had occasioned. During a conversation in the streets of Philadelphia immediately after retiring from Mr. Hamilton's house. Mr. Venable repeated to me, that the explanation was entirely satisfactory, and expressed his concern, that he had been a party to whom it had been made. Though in the course of the conversation Mr. Venable expressed his discontent with public measures which had been recommended by Mr. Hamilton, yet he manifested a high respect for his Talents, and confidence in the integrity of his character.

When Mr. Reynolds was in Prison, it was reported to me, that he had threatened to make disclosures injurious to the character of some head of a Department. This report I communicated to Mr. Hamilton, who advised me to take no steps towards a liberation of Reynolds while such a report existed and remained unexplained. This was antecedent to the interview between Mr. Hamilton and Messrs. Monroe, Muhlenberg and Venable, or to any knowledge on my part of the circumstance by which it was occasioned.

The Offence for which Reynolds and Clingman were prosecuted by my direction, was for suborning a person to commit perjury for the purpose of obtaining Letters of Administration on the estate of a person who was living. After the prosecution was commenced, Clingman confessed to me, that he and Reynolds were possessed of lists of the names and sums due to certain Creditors of the United States, which lists had been obtained from the Treasury—Both Clingman and Reynolds obstinately refused for some time to deliver up the lists or to disclose the name of the person, through whose infidelity they had been obtained. At length on receiving a promise from me, that I would endeavour to effect their liberation from the consequences of the prosecution, they consented to surrender the lists, to restore the balance which had been fraudulently obtained, and to reveal the name of the person, by whom the lists had been furnished.

This was done conformably to the proposition contained in a letter from Clingman dated December 4, 1792, of which a copy is hereunto annexed. The original letter and the lists which were surrendered now remain in my possession. Agreeably to my engagement I informed Jared Ingersol Esqr. Attorney General of Pennsylvania, that an important discovery had been made, and the condition by which it could be rendered useful to the public in preventing future frauds; in consequence of which the prosecutions against Clingman and Reynolds were dismissed.

In the publication referred to, it is suggested that the lists were furnished by Mr. Duer; this is an injurious mistake—nothing occurred at any time to my knowledge, which could give colour to a suspicion, that Mr. Duer was in any manner directly or indirectly concerned with or privy to the transaction. The infidelity was committed by a clerk in the office of the Register—Mr. Duer resigned his office in March, 1790, while the Treasury was at New York—the Clerk who furnished the lists was first employed in Philadelphia in January 1791. The Accounts from which the lists were taken, were all settled at the Treasury subsequent to the time last mentioned; on the discovery above stated the Clerk was dismissed, and has not since been employed in the public offices. The name of the Clerk who was dismissed has not been publicly mentioned, for a reason which appears in Clingman's letter; but if the disclosure is found necessary to the vindication of an innocent character it shall be made.

Certified in Philadelphia, this twelfth day of July, 1797.

OLIV. WOLCOTT.

Copy of a letter from Jacob Clingman, to the Comptroller of the Treasury.

Phila. 4 December, 1792.

Sir

Having unfortunately for myself, been brought into a very disagreeable situation, on account of Letters of Administration taken out by a certain John Delabar on the effects of a certain Ephraim Goodanough, who, it since appears, is still living. I beg leave to mention that I am ready to refund the money to the Treasury or to the proper owner or his order, and if it can be of any service to the Treasury Department or to the United States, in giving up the lists of the names of the persons to whom pay is due, and to disclose the name of the person in the utmost confidence from whom the list was obtained, earnestly hoping that may be some inducement to withdraw the action against me, which if prosecuted can only end in injuring my character without any further advantage to the United States.

I have the honor to be
your most humble Servant
Signed,
Jacob Clingman.
Hon. Oliver Wolcott, Esq.

No. XXV.
New-York July 5, 1797.
Sir,

In a pamphlet lately published entitled. "No. V. of the History of the United States for 1796 &c." are sundry papers respecting the affair of *Reynolds*, in which you once had an agency, accompanied with these among other comments. "They [certain attacks on Mr. Monroe] are ungrateful, because he displayed on an occasion, that will be mentioned immediately, the greatest lenity to Mr. Alexander Hamilton, the prime mover of the Federal party. When some of the papers which are now to be laid before the world were submitted to the Secretary; when he was informed that they were to be communicated to President Washington he entreated in the most anxious tone of deprecation that the measure might be suspended. Mr. Monroe was one of the three gentlemen who agreed to this delay. They gave their consent to it on his express promise of a guarded behaviour in future, and because he attached to the suppression of these papers a mysterious degree of solicitude which they feeling no personal resentment against the individual, were unwilling to augment." Page 204 and 205. It is also suggested page 206 that I made "a volunteer acknowledgment of *seduction*" and it must be understood from the context that this acknowledgment was made to the same three gentlemen.

The peculiar nature of this transaction renders it impossible that you should not recollect it in all its parts and that your own declaration to me at the time contradicts absolutely the construction which the editor of the Pamphlet puts upon the affair.

I think myself entitled to ask from your candour and justice a declaration equivalent to that which was made me at the time in the presence of Mr. Wolcott by yourself and the two other gentlemen accompanied by a contradiction of the representations in the comments cited above—And I shall rely upon your delicacy that the manner of doing it will be such as one gentleman has a right to expect from another—especially as you must be sensible that the present appearance of the papers is contrary to the course which was understood between us to be proper, and includes a dishonourable infidelity somewhere—I am far from attributing it to either of the three gentlemen; yet the suspicion naturally falls on some agent made use of by them.

I send you the copy of a Memorandum of the substance of your declaration, made by me the morning after our interview.

With consideration
I have the honor to be,
Sir,
Your very obed. servt.
Alexander Hamilton.

P. S. I must beg the favour of expedition in your reply.
Memorandum of Substance of Declaration of Messrs. Monroe, Muhlenberg and Venable concerning the affair of J. Reynolds.

That they regretted the trouble and uneasiness which they had occasioned to me in consequence of the representations made to them—That they were perfectly satisfied with the explanation I had given and that there was nothing in the transaction which ought to affect my character as a public officer or lessen the public confidence in my integrity.

No. XXVI.
Philadelphia, December, 1792.
Gentlemen,

On reflection, I deem it advisable for me to have Copies of the several papers which you communicated to me in our interview on Saturdey evening, including the notes, and the fragment of Mr. Reynolds' letter to Mr. Clingman. I therefore request that you will either cause copies of these papers to be furnished to me, taken by the person in whose hand-writing the declarations which you shewed to me were, or will let me have the papers themselves to be copied. It is also my wish, that all such papers as are original may be detained from the parties of whom they were, had, to put it out of their power repeat the abuse of them in situations which may deprive, me of the advantage of explanation. Considering of how abominable an attempt they have been the instruments, I trust you will feel no scruples about this detention.

With consideration,
I have the honour to be,
Gentlemen,
Your obedient Servant,

ALEXANDER HAMILTON.

F. Augustus Muhlenberg,
James Monroe, and } Esquires.
Abraham Venable,

No. XXVII.
Philad. December 18th. 1792.
Sir,
I have communicated your letter of yesterday to Messrs. Venables and Monroe. The latter has all the papers relating to the subject in his possession, and I have the pleasure to inform you that your very reasonable request

will be speedily complied with. I have the honor to be, with much esteem.

Your most obedient,
Humble Serv't,
FREDK. A. MUHLENBERG.
Alexander Hamilton, Esq.

No. XXVIII.
Sir,

I have the honor to enclose you copies of the papers requested in yours a few days past—That of the notes you will retain; the others you will be pleased, after transcribing, to return me.

With due respect, I have the honor to be,
Your very humble Servant,
JAS. MONROE.

Every thing you desire in the letter above-mentioned shall be most strictly complied with.

Philadelphia, Dec. 20, 1792.
The Hon. Alexander Hamilton, Esq.
Philadelphia.

No. XXIX.
Philadelphia, July 10th, 1797.
Sir,

As I not reside in the city at present, your letter of the 5th inst. did not reach me time enough to answer by

Saturday's post. Whilst I lament the publication of the papers respecting the affair of Reynolds (of which I hope I need not assure you that I had neither knowledge or agency, for I never saw them since the affair took place, nor was I ever furnished with a copy) I do not hesitate to declare that I regretted the trouble and uneasiness this business had occasioned, and that I was perfectly satisfied with the explanation you gave. At the same time permit me to remind you of your declaration also made in the presence of Mr. Wolcott that the information and letters in our possession justified the suspicions we entertained before your explanation took place, and that our conduct towards you in this business was satisfactory Having no share or agency whatever in the publication or comments you are pleased to cite I must beg to be excused from making any remarks thereon. Were I to undertake to contradict the many absurdities and falsehoods which I see published on a variety of subjects which heretofore came under my notice, it would require more time than I am willing to sacrifice.

I have the honor to be

Sir,

Your obedt. humble servt.

Fredk. A. Muhlenberg.

A. Hamilton, Esq.

No. XXX.

Philadelphia, July 9th, 1797.

Sir

I have received your letter of the fifth instant by the hands of Mr. Wolcott.

I had heard of the pamphlet you mention some days before, but had not read it. I am entirely ignorant of the Editor, and of the means by which he procured the papers alluded to.

I have had nothing to do with the transaction since the interview with you, I do not possess a copy of the papers at present, nor have I at any time had the possession of any of them, I avoided taking a copy because I feared that the greatest care which I could exercise in keeping them safely, might be defeated by some accident and that some person or other might improperly obtain an inspection of them. I have endeavoured to recollect what passed at the close of the interview which took place with respect to this transaction; it was said I believe by us in general terms, that we were satisfied with the explanation that had been given, that we regretted the necessity we had been subjected to in being obliged to make the inquiry, as well as the trouble and anxiety it bad occasioned you, and on your part you admitted in general terms that the business as presented to us bore such a doubtful aspect as to justify the inquiry, and that the manner had been satisfactory to you.

I have now to express my surprise at the contents of a letter published yesterday in Fenno's paper, in which you endeavour to impute to party motives, the part which I have had in this business, and endeavour to connect me with the releasement of persons *committed as you say for heinous crimes.* Clingman had been released before I heard of the business, and Reynolds on the very day I received the first intimation of it, arrangements having been previously made for that purpose, by those who had interested themselves to bring it about, so that no application was made to me on that subject, either directly or indirectly the object being entirely accomplished by other means, and before I was informed of their confinement; If you will take the trouble to examine the transaction you will find this statement correct, and you cannot be insensible of the injury you do me when you say, this was an attempt to release themselves from imprisonment by favor of party spirit, and that I was one of the persons resorted to on that ground. I appeal to your candour, and ask you if any part of my conduct in this whole business has justified such an imputation. This having been a joint business and Mr. Monroe living now in New-York, I must avoid saying any thing more on this

subject until I can see him and Mr. Muhlenberg together, which I hope will be in the present week.

I am Sir Humble Servant

Abm. B. Venable

No. XXXII.

ME. Monroe has the honor to inform Col. Hamilton that he arrived in this city yesterday A, M. 12—That Mr. Muhlenberg and himself are to have a meeting this morning upon the subject which concerns him, and after which Col. Hamilton shall immediately hear from them.

Monday morning, July 16, 1797.

No. XXXIII.
Philadelphia, July 17, 1797.
Sir,

It was our wish to have given a joint answer with Mr. Venable to your favour of the 5th instant concerning the publication of the proceedings in an inquiry in which we were jointly engaged with him in 1792, respecting an affair between yourself and Mr. Reynolds; and into which, from the circumstances attending it, we deemed it our duty to enquire. His departure however for Virginia precludes the possibility of so doing at present. We nevertheless readily give such explanation upon that point as we are now able to give; the original papers having been deposited in the hands of a respectable character in Virginia soon after the transaction took place, and where they now are.

We think proper to observe that as we had no agency

in or knowledge of the publication of these papers till they appeared, so of course we could have none in the comments that were made on them.

But you particularly wish to know what the impression was which your explanation of that affair made on our minds, in the interview we had with you upon that subject at your own house, as stated in the paper No. 5, of the publication referred to; and to which we readily reply, that the impression which we left in your mind as stated in that number, was that which rested on our own, and which was that the explanation of the nature of your connection with Reynolds which you then gave removed the suspicions we had before entertained of your being connected with him in speculation. Had not this been the case we should certainly not have left that impression on your mind, nor should we have desisted from the plan we had contemplated in the commencement of the inquiry, of laying the papers before the President of the U. States.

We presume that the papers to which our signatures are annexed are in all cases correct. 'Tis proper however to observe that as the notes contained in No. 5. were intended only as memoranda of the explanation which you gave us in that interview, as likewise the information which was afterwards given us by Mr. Clingham on the same subject, and without a view to any particular use, they were entered concisely and without form. This is sufficiently obvious from the difference which appears in that respect, between the papers which preceded our interview and those contained in No. 5, of the publication.

We cannot conclude this letter without expressing our surprize at the contents of a paper in the Gazette of the United States of the 8th instant, which states that the proceedings in the inquiry in question, were the contrivance of two very profligate men who sought to obtain their liberation from prison by the favor of party spirit. You will readily recollect that one of those men Mr. Clingham was never imprisoned for any crime alledged against him by the department of the Treasury, and that the other Mr. Reynolds was upon the point of being released and was actually released and without our solicitation or even wish, by virtue of an agreement made with him by that department before the inquiry began. We feel too very sensibly the injustice of the intimation that any of us were influenced by party spirit, because we well know that such was not the case: nor can we otherwise than be the more surprized that such an intimation should now be given, since we well remember that our conduct upon that occasion excited your sensibility, and obtained from you an unequivocal acknowledgment of our candour.

With consideration we are, Sir,
your most obedient
and very humble servants,
Fredk. A. Muhlenberg.
Jas. Monroe.

No. XXXIV.

Gentlemen,

I have your letter of this date. It gives me pleasure to receive your explanation of the ambiguous phrase in the paper No. V. published with your signatures and that of Mr. Venable, and your information of the fact, that my explanation had been satisfactory to you.

You express your surprize at the contents of a paper in the Gazette of the U. States of the 8th instant. If you will review that paper with care, you will find, that what is said about *party spirit* refers to the view with which the accusation was instituted by Reynolds and Clingman, not to that with which the inquiry was entered into by you. They sought by the *favor of party spirit* to obtain liberation from prison—but tho' they may have rested their hopes on this ground it is not said, nor in my opinion implied, that you in making the inquiry were actuated by that spirit—I cannot however alter my opinion that they were influenced by the motive ascribed to them—For though, as you observe Clingman was not in prison (and so far my memory has erred) and though it be true, that Reynolds was released before the inquiry began by virtue of an agreement with the Treasury Department (that is the Comptroller of the Treasury) for a reason of public utility which has been explained to you,—Yet it will be observed that Clingman as well as Reynolds was actually under a prosecution for the same offence, and that it appears by No. I. of the papers under your signatures, than for a period of more than three weeks while *Clingman* was in the act of soliciting the "*aid and friendship of Mr. Muhlenberg on behalf of himself and Reynolds to get them released or discharged from the prosecution*" he Clingman frequently dropped hints to

Mr. Muhlenberg, that Reynolds had it in his power *very materially to injure the secretary of the Treasury* and that *Reynolds knew several very improper transactions of his;*— and at last went so far as to state that *Reynolds said he had it in his power to hang the secretary of the Treasury* who was *deeply concerned in speculation*." From this it appears, that the suggestions to my prejudice were early made, and were connected with the endeavour to obtain relief through Mr. Muhlenberg—I derive from all this a confirmation of my opinion founded on the general nature of the proceeding that *Reynolds* and *Clingman*, knowing the existence in Congress of a party hostile to my conduct in administration, and that the newspapers devoted to it, frequently contained insinuations of my being concerned in improper speculations, formed upon that basis the plan of conciliating the favour and aid of that party towards getting rid of the prosecution by accusing me of Speculation. This is what I meant in the publication alluded to and what I must always believe.

With this explanation, you will be sensible that there is nothing in the publication inconsistent with my declaration to you at closing our interview. It is very true, that after the full and unqualified expressions which came from you together with Mr. Venable, differing in terms but agreeing in substance, of your entire satisfaction, with the explanation I had given, and that there was nothing in the affair of the nature suggested; accompanied with expressions of regret at the trouble and anxiety occasioned to me—and when (as I recollect it) some one of the gentlemen expressed a hope that the manner of conducting the inquiry had appeared to me fair and liberal—I replied in substance that though I had been displeased with the mode of introducing the subject to me (which you will remember I manifested at the time in very lively terms) yet that in other respects I was satisfied with and sensible to the candour with which I had been treated. And this was the sincere impression of my mind.

With Consideration
I am Gentlemen
Your most Obedt. and hum. serv.
Alexander Hamilton.

No. XXXV.
Sir,
I send herewith an answer to the joint letter of Mr. Muhlenberg and yourself. It appears to me on reflection requisite to have some explanation on the note of January 2, 1793, with your signature only. It may be inferred from

the attention to record the information of Clingman therein stated after what had passed between us that you meant to give credit and sanction to the suggestion that the defence set up by me was an imposition—You will, I doubt not, be sensible of the propriety of my requesting you to explain yourself on this point also.

I remain with consideration

Sir your obedient servant

Alexander Hamilton

No. XXXVI.

Philadelphia, July 17, 1797.

Sir,

It is impossible for me to trace back at this moment, occupied as I am with other concerns, all the impressions of my mind at the different periods at which the memoranda were made in the publication to which you refer in your favour of to-day, but I well remember that in entering the one which bears my single signature, altho' I was surprized at the communication given, yet I neither meant to give or imply any opinion of my own as to its contents. I simply entered the communication as I received it, reserving to myself the liberty to form an opinion upon it at such future time as I found convenient, paying due regard to all the circumstances connected with it.

I am Sir with consideration
your very humble servant
James Monroe.

No. XXXVII.

Sir,

Your letter of yesterday in answer to mine of the same date was received last night. I am sorry to say, that as I understand it, it is unsatisfactory—It appears to me liable to this inference that the information of Clingman had revived the suspicions which my explanation had removed. This would include the very derogatory suspicion, that I had concerted with Reynolds not only the fabrication of all the letters and documents under his hand but also the forgery of the letters produced as those of Mrs. Reynolds—since these last unequivocally contradict the pretence communicated by Clingman. I therefore request you to say whether this inference be intended.

With Consideration, I am. Sir,
Your very obedient servant,
Alexander Hamilton.
July 18, 1797.
James Monroe, Esqr.

No. XXXVIII.
Philadelphia, July 18, 1797.
Sir

I can only observe that in entering the note which bears my single signature I did not convey or mean to convey any opinion of my own, as to the faith which was due to it, but left it to stand on its own merits reserving to myself the right to judge of it, as upon any fact afterwards communicated according to its import and authenticity.

With due respect I am Sir

Your very humble servant

James Monroe.

No. XXXIX.
July 20, 1797.
Sir,

In my last letter to you I proposed a simple and direct question, to which I had hoped an answer equally simple and direct. That which I have received, though amounting, if I understand it, to an answer in the negative, is conceived in such circuitous terms as may leave an obscurity upon the point which ought not to have remained. In this situation, I feel it proper to tell you frankly my impression of the matter.

The having any communication with Clingman, after that with me, receiving from him and recording information depending on the mere veracity of a man undeniably guilty of subornation of perjury, and one whom the very documents which he himself produced to you shewed sufficiently[2] to be the accomplice of a vindictive attempt upon me, the leaving it in a situation where by possibility, it might rise up at a future and remote day to inculpate me, without the possibility perhaps from the lapse of time of establishing the refutation, and all this without my privity or knowledge, was in my opinion in a high degree indelicate and improper. To have given or intended to give the least sanction or credit after all that was known to you, to the mere assertion of either of the three persons *Clingman*, *Reynolds* or his wife would have betrayed a disposition towards me which if it appeared exist would merit epithets the severest that I could apply.

With consideration I am Sir,
your very humble servant
Alexander Hamilton.
James Monroe, Esq.

No. XL.
Philadelphia, July 21, 1797.
Sir

---

[2] See the letter from Reynolds to Clingman in which he declares that he will have satisfaction of me at all events and that he trusts only to Clingman.

Your favour of yesterday (to use your own language) gives an indelicate and improper colouring to the topic to which it refers. I will endeavour in a few words to place the points in discussion where they ought to stand.

It was never our intention other than to fulfill our duty to the public, in our inquiry into your conduct, and with *delicacy* and *propriety* to yourself nor have we done otherwise.

To this truth, in respect to the inquiry, as to our conduct upon that occasion, you have so often assented, that nothing need now be said on that point. Indeed I should have considered myself as highly criminal, advised as I was of your conduct, had I not united in the inquiry into it: for what offence can be more reprehensible in an officer charged with the finances of his country, than to be engaged in speculation? And what other officer who had reason to suspect this could justify himself for failing to examine into the truth of this charge? We did so—apprized you of what we had done—heard your explanation and were satisfied with it. It is proper to observe that in the explanation you gave, you admitted all the facts upon which our opinion was founded, but yet accounted for them, and for your connection with Reynolds on another principle. Tis proper also to observe that we admitted your explanation upon the faith of your own statement, and upon the documents you presented, though I do not recollect they were proved or that proof was required of them.

You will remember that in this interview in which we acknowledged ourselves satisfied with the explanation you gave, we did not bind ourselves not to hear further information on the subject, or even not to proceed further in case we found it our duty so to do. This would have been improper, because subsequent facts might be disclosed which might change our opinion and in which case it would be our duty to proceed further. And with respect to Mr. Clingman we thought it highly proper to hear what he had to say, because we had before heard him on the subject, and because you had acknowledged all his previous information to be true, and because he was a party and had a right to be heard on it. You observe by the entry that we did not seek him, nor even apprize him of the explanation received from you, on the contrary that he sought us and in consequence of information received from Mr. Wolcott.

The subject is now before the public, and I repeat to you what I have said before, that I do not wish any opinion of my own to be understood as conveyed in the entry which bears my single signature, because when I entered it I had no opinion upon it, as sufficiently appears by my subsequent conduct, having never acted upon it, and deposited the papers with a friend when I left my country, in whose hands they still are. Whether the imputations against you as to speculation, are well or ill founded, depends upon the facts and circumstances which appear against you upon your defence. If you shew that they are ill founded, I shall he contented, for I have never undertaken to accuse you since our interview, nor do I now give any opinion on it, reserving to myself the liberty to form one, after I see your defence; being resolved, however, so far as depends on me, not to bar the door to free inquiry as to the merits of the case in either view.

This contains a just state of this affair so far as I remember it, which I presume will be satisfactory to you: and to which I shall only add that as on the one hand I shall always be ready to do justice to the claims of any one upon me, so I shall always be equally prepared to vindicate my conduct and character against the attacks of any one who may assail them.

With due respect, I am Sir,

Your obedient servant,

James Monroe.

No. XLI.

City of Philadelphia, ss.

Mary Williams of the City aforesaid Boarding House Keeper maketh Oath that She is acquainted with Mrs. M. Reynolds formerly reputed to be the Wife of Mr. James Reynolds that her acquaintance commenced by the said Mrs. Reynolds calling upon her to obtain admission as a lodger which the Deponent declined that afterwards the Deponent frequently saw the said Mrs. Reynolds and also frequently saw her write that from this she the Deponent conceives herself to be well acquainted with the hand writing of the said Mrs. Reynolds and is well satisfied that the hand writing of the letters hereunto

annexed numbered

I—VIII—IX—X—XII—XIII is of the proper hand writing of the said Mrs. Reynolds to indentify which letters the more particularly this Deponent hath upon each of them endorsed her name.

Sworn this XXIst day of
July MDCCXCVII. be-   } Mary Williams
before me

Robert Wharton
One of the Aldermen of the
City of Philadelphia.

No. XLII.
Wednesday 5th, December, 1792.
Honnoured Sir,

too well you are acquainted with my unfortenate setuvation, to give you an explanation thereof, I am informed by a Note from Mrs. Reynolds this Evening, wherein She informed Me that you have bin informed, that I Should have Said, if I were not discharged in two days, that I would make Some of the heads of the Departments tremble, now Sir I declare to god, that I never have said any Such thing, nor never have I said any thing, against any Head of a department whatever, all I have Said, Sir. is that I am under the Necessaty of letting you Know, which of the Clarks in the publick Office has givein out the List, of the ballance due. from the United States, to the individual States, and when it

Comes to your knowledge, that the would tremble. Now Can I have an Enemy So base as to lodge such False allegations to my Charge, which is tottely Groundless, and without the least foundation Immaginable. now Sir, if you will give me the pleashure of waiting uppon your honour tomorrow I will give you every information that lies in my power Respecting the Matter, which I hope it will give you final Satisfaction, what I have done never Was with a wish to Rong the United States or any Other person whatever, the person that Administer On this mans pay. which he Received from the United States, had my monies in his hands and would not transfer the Certificate to Mrs. Clingman and myself untill wee signed the bond of indamnification. to him now dear Sir. that was our Situvation. to Secure our own Interest, wee executed the Bond, which was an Oversight of ours, now Sir Can you Suppose In my present Setuvation, that I would say any thing against you Sir or any Other head of department whatever, where it even was in my power which was not. Espicially where all my hopes and Dependance where, now dear Sir, think of my poor innocent, family, not of me, for them I Onely wish to live

I am, honnored Sir

Your most Obediant and

Humble Servt.

James W, Reynolds

Oliver Woolcot Esqr.

No. XLIII.

Having seen in a pamphlet published in Philadelphia entitled "The History of the United States No. 5" a paragraph to the following Effect:

"During the late Canvass for the Election of a President, Webster, in his Minerva, gave a Hint that Mr. Hamilton would be an adviseable Candidate. A person in this City who chanced to see this Newspaper, wrote immediately to a correspondent in New-York. The letter desired him to put himself in the way of Mr. Hamilton and inform him that, if Webster should in future print a single paragraph on that Head, the papers referred to were instantly to be laid before the World. The Message was delivered to Mr. Hamilton and the Minerva became silent."

I declare that the contents of the foregoing paragraph, as far as they relate to myself, are totally *false*. I never entertained an idea that Mr. Hamilton was a Candidate for the Presidency or Vice-Presidency at the late Election.—I never uttered, wrote or published a Hint or Suggestion of the kind; nor did I ever receive from Mr. Hamilton or any other person either directly or indirectly, any Hint or Communication to discontinue any notice or Suggestions on that subject. I have examined the Minerva for several months previous to the late Election, and I cannot find a Suggestion published in that paper, of Mr. Hamilton's being a Candidate as aforesaid, either from any Correspondent or republished from any other paper; nor have I the least knowledge what the suggestions in the foregoing paragraph allude to.

My own idea uniformly was, that Mr. Adams and Mr. Pinckney were the only Candidates supported by Mr. Hamilton and the friends of our Government in general.

Sworn the 13th, July 1797.
before me Abm. Skinner N. P. } Noah Webster Jun.

No. XLIV.
Philadelphia, June 27, 1797.
Sir,

It would have highly gratified me had it been in my power to furnish the relief you ask: but I am preparing for my departure and find, on-winding up my affairs, that I shall not have one dollar to spare. It is therefore with sincere regret I have nothing better to tender than the sentiments of good will of
Sir,
Your most obedient servant,
Th. Jefferson.

No. XLV.
Philadelphia, June 28, 1797.
Sir,

I know well that you were a clerk in the Treasury Department while I was in the office of Secretary of State;

but as I had no relation with the interior affairs of that office, I had no opportunity of being acquainted with you personally, except the single occasion on which you called on me. The length of time you were in the office affords the best presumption in your favour, and the particular misunderstanding which happened to you with your principals may account for your not having obtained from them those certificates of character which I am not able to supply. I doubt not however that a knowledge of your conduct wherever you establish yourself will soon render all certificates unnecessary, and I sincerely wish you may obtain employment which may evince and reward good conduct.

I am, Sir,

Your very humble servant,

Th. Jefferson.

No. XLVI

Sir,

I have maturely considered your letter of yesterday delivered to me at about nine last night and cannot find in it cause of satisfaction.

There appears to me in the first place an attempt to prop the veracity of Clingman by an assertion which is not correct, namely that I had acknowledged all his previous information to be true. This was not and could not be the fact—I acknowledged parts of it to be true but certainly not the whole—on the contrary, I am able to prove that a material part of it, according to its obvious intent, is false, and I know other parts of it to be so— Indeed in one sense I could not have made the acknowledgment alledged without acknowledging myself guilty.

In the second place there appears a design at all events to drive me to the necessity of a formal defence while you know that the extreme delicacy of its nature must be very disagreeable to me. It is my opinion that as you have been the cause, no matter how, of the business appearing in a shape which gives it an adventitious importance, and this against the intent of a Confidence reposed in you by me, as contrary to what was delicate and proper, you recorded Clingman's testimony without my privity and thereby gave it countenance, as I had given you an explanation with which you was satisfied and which could leave no doubt upon a candid mind it was incumbent upon you as a man of honour and sensibility to have come forward in a manner that would have shielded me completely from the unpleasant effects brought upon me by your agency. This you have not done.

On the contrary, by the affected reference of the matter to a defence which I am to make, and by which you profess your opinion is to be decided—you imply that your suspicions are still alive. And as nothing appears to have shaken your original conviction but the wretched tale of Clingman, which you have thought fit to record, it follows that you are pleased to attach a degree of weight to that Communication which cannot be accounted for on any fair principles. The result in my mind is that you have been and are actuated by motives towards me malignant and dishonourable; nor can I doubt that this will be the universal opinion when the publication of the whole affair which I am about to make shall be seen.

I am Sir,

your humble Servant,

Alexr, Hamilton.

Philadelphia July 22. 1797.

J. Monroe Esqr.

No. XLVII.

Philadelphia, July 25th, 1797.

Sir,

I received your letter of the 22d instant by Major Jackson and have paid it the attention it merits.

Always anxious to do justice to every one, it would afford me pleasure could I answer it in a manner satisfactory to your feelings: but while the respect which I owe to myself forbids me replying in that harsh stile which you have adopted, that same respect with an attention to truth, according to the impressions existing on my mind, will compel me upon all occasions to place this affair on its true ground.

Why you have adopted this stile I know not. If your object is to render this affair a personal one between us you might have been more explicit, since you well know, if that is your disposition, what my determination is, and to which I shall firmly adhere. But if it is to illustrate truth and place the question on its true merits, as I have always been disposed to do, it appears illy calculated to promote that end.

I have constantly said and I repeat again that in making an entry which appears after our interview with you, and which ought to have been signed by the other gentlemen as well as myself I never intended to convey an opinion upon it, nor does it convey any opinion of my own, but merely notes what Clingman stated, leaving it upon his own credit only. But you wish me to state that this communication made no impression on my mind, and this I shall not state because in so doing I should be incorrect. On the other hand, I do not wish to be understood as intimating that this communication had absolutely changed my opinion, for in that event I should have acted on it, whereas, the contrary was the case as you well know. And with respect to the propriety of noting down that communication, I have no doubt on that point, since I should have noted any other that might have been made on the same topic by that or any other party. Indeed if it was proper to note the communications first received, it was equally so to note this, and *that* you did not disapprove. Had we proceeded in it you may be well assured we should have apprised of it, as in the other case, as well as from motives of candour towards you, as propriety on our own parts.

It is not my wish to discuss the fact whether you admitted all or only parts of Clingman's communication in our interview with you, because upon the principle in which I stand engaged in this affair not as your accuser, but called on to explain, it is one of no importance to me. Such was the impression upon my mind; if however the contrary were the case, and you shewed to be so, I should be equally contented as if it were otherwise, since it is my wish that truth appear in her genuine character, upon the present, as upon all other occasions.

I am. Sir, with due respect

Your obedient servant,

James Monroe.

No. XLVIII.

New York, July 28, 1797.

Sir,

Your letter of the 25th instant reached me yesterday. Without attempting to analize the precise import of your expressions, in that particular, and really at a loss for your meaning when you appeal to my knowledge of a determination to which you say you should firmly adhere, I shall observe, in relation to the idea of my desiring to make the affair personal between us, that it would be no less unworthy of me to seek than to shun such an issue.—It was my earnest wish to have experienced a conduct on your part, such as was in my opinion due to me, to yourself, and to justice. Thinking as I did on the coolest reflection, that this had not been the case, I did not hesitate to convey to you the impressions which I entertained, prepared for any consequences to which it might lead.

Nevertheless, it would have been agreeable to me to have found in your last letter sufficient cause for relinquishing those impressions. But I cannot say that I do—The idea is every way inadmissible, that *Clingman's* last miserable contrivance should have had weight to shake, though not *absolutely change* the opinion which my explanation had produced; and that having such an effect it should have been recorded and preserved in secret without the slightest intimation to me. There was a vast difference between what might have been proper before and after my explanation; though I am not disposed to admit, that the attention which was paid to such characters, even before, would have been justifiable, had it not been for the notes in my handwriting.

But the subject is too disgusting to leave me any inclination to prolong this discussion of it. The public explanation to which I am driven must decide, as far as public opinion is concerned, between us. Painful as the appeal will be in one respect, I know that in the principal point, it must completely answer my purpose. I am, Sir,

Your humble servant,

Alexander Hamilton.

No. XLIX,
Philadelphia, July 31, 1797.
Sir,
Your letter of the 28th which I have received claims a short answer.

I have stated to you that I have no wish to do you a personal injury. The several explanations which I have made accorded with truth and my ideas of propriety. Therefore I need not repeat them. If these do not yield you satisfaction, I can give no other, unless called on in a way which for the illustration of truth, I wish to avoid, but which I am ever ready to meet. This is what I meant by that part of my letter which you say you do not understand.

With due respect I am Sir,
Your humble servant,
JAS. MONROE.
Alexander Hamilton, Esq.

No. L.
(Copy) *New-York, August* 4, 1797.
Sir,
In my opinion the idea of a personal affair between us ought not to have found a place in your letters or it ought to have assumed a more positive shape. In the state to

which our correspondence had brought the question, it lay with you to make the option whether such an issue should take place. If what you have said be intended as an advance towards it, it is incumbent upon me not to decline it. On the supposition that it is so intended, I have authorized Major Jackson to communicate with you and to settle time and place.

I am Sir, Your humble servt.

Alexander Hamilton.

James Munroe Esq.

No. LI.

Philadelphia, August, 6, 1797.

Sir,

I do not clearly understand the import of your letter of the 4th instant and therefore desire an explanation. With this view I will give an explanation of mine which preceded.

Seeing no adequate cause by any thing in our late correspondence, why I should give a challenge to you, I own it was not my intention to give or even provoke one by any thing contained in those letters. I meant only to observe that I should stand on the defensive and receive one in case you thought fit to give it. If therefore you were under a contrary impression, I frankly own you are mistaken. If on the other hand you meant this last letter as a challenge to me, I have then to request that you will say so, and in which case have to inform you that my friend Col. Burr who will present you this and who will communicate with you on the subject is authorized to give my answer to it, and to make such other arrangements as may be suit, able in such an event.

With due respect I am

Your very humble servt.

A. Hamilton Esq. James Monroe.

No. LII.

New-York, Aug. 9, 1797.

Sir,

The intention of my letter of the 4th instant as itself imports, was to meet and close with an advance towards a personal interview, which it appeared to me had been made by you.

From the tenor of your reply of the 6th, which disavows the inference I had drawn, any further step on my part, as being inconsistent with the ground I have heretofore taken, would be improper,

I am Sir, your humble servant,

Alexander Hamilton.

James Monroe Esq.

N. B. It may be proper to observe that in addition to the original letters from Mrs. Reynolds, there are in the hands of the gentlemen with whom the papers are deposited, two original letters from her, one addressed to Mr. R. Folwell—the other to a Mrs. Miller, and both of them signed MARIA CLINGMAN, in the former of which she mentions the circumstance of her being married to Clingman.

TIMELINE

YEAR	EVENT
1755 or 1757	• Born on the island of Nevis in the West Indies (January 11)
1765	• The family moves to the island of St. Croix
	• Father James abandons the family soon thereafter
1766	• Clerks at the St. Croix Counting House for Nicholas Cruger
1768	• Mother Rachel dies (February 18)
	• Nearly dies from the same disease
1773	• Local leaders raise funds for Hamilton to travel to America to study
1774	• Attends King's College (now Columbia University)
	• Writes first political essay "Full Vindication of the Measures of Congress," which supports the boycott of English goods
1775	• Intervenes when a tea party mob attempts to attack Myles Cooper, the president of King's College, and saves his life
1776	• Commissioned as a captain in the 5th Field Artillery
	• Fights at the Battle of Long Island (Battle of Brooklyn)

1776 (cont.)	• Crosses the Delaware River with Gen. Washington and fights at Trenton
1777	• Fights at the Battle of Princeton
	• Promoted by Gen. Washington to Lt. Colonel and aide-de-camp
1778	• Fights at the Battle of Monmouth
1779	• Writes to John Jay, the president of the Continental Congress, proposing the establishment of black battalions and offering freedom for those who serve
1780	• Marries Elizabeth Schuyler (December 14)
1781	• Argument with Gen. Washington creates a temporary rift between the two friends; Hamilton leaves his command and goes home
	• Returns to lead the victory at the Battle of Yorktown
1782	• First of eight children, Philip, born (January 22)
	• Refuses military pay and pension
	• Selected as a representative to the Continental Congress from New York
1783	• Treaty of Paris ends the Revolutionary War
	• Moves to a home on Wall Street in New York City
1784	• Opposes violence against former Tories and loyalists
	• As an attorney, takes the first of many cases against the Trespass Act, helping to shape the nation's legal code and promoting reconciliation with the British and their supporters
1785	• Leads a failed attempt to end slavery
1786	• Elected to the New York State Legislature
	• Appointed delegate to the Annapolis Convention
	• Drafts the Convention's report

1787	• Delegate to the Constitutional Convention in Philadelphia
	• Leader of the New York delegation; key framer of the Constitution
	• Signs Constitution
	• Starts writing the Federalist Papers (authors 51 of 85 of the essays that helped ratify the Constitution)
1788	• Leads the effort at the New York Convention that ratifies the Constitution
1789	• Named Treasury Secretary by President George Washington
	• Starts developing a plan to address the war debt and establish the nation's financial system
1790	• Issues first public report on the nation's finances and public credit
	• Joins Thomas Jefferson and James Madison at a famous dinner, where he forges the compromises for the location of the nation's capital city and debt assumption
	• Proposes to Congress the establishment of a national bank
1791	• Given the opposition to his financial plans and the bank, Hamilton advocates notion of "implied powers" in the Constitution
	• Begins his affair with Maria Reynolds
1792	• Republicans falsely accuse Hamilton of financial impropriety and investigate him
1793	• Convinces President Washington to remain neutral in the war between Britain and France
	• Yellow fever epidemic strikes Philadelphia; Hamilton and his family remain in the city, become ill, but survive

1794
- Leads the military and political suppression of the Whiskey Rebellion in western Pennsylvania

1795
- Issues another financial report and series of proposals to Congress
- Resigns as Treasury Secretary
- Returns to New York City to practice law

1796
- Helps President Washington draft his famous Farewell Address

1797
- Infamous pamphlet by James Callender accuses Hamilton of an affair with Maria Reynolds and various financial improprieties

1798
- Tensions with France necessitate Gen. Washington advising President Adams to appoint Hamilton as head of the army

1799
- Father James dies
- George Washington dies

1800
- Helps broker the controversial end to the Electoral College tie and impasse between Thomas Jefferson and Aaron Burr, giving the presidency to Jefferson
- Starts building his home "The Grange" in upper Manhattan

1801
- Co-founds the Federalist newspaper *The New York Evening Post*
- Son Philip is shot at Weehawken, New Jersey in a duel with George Eacker, a man who defamed Hamilton's character, and dies the next day of his wounds

1802	• Moves family to "The Grange"
1804	• Helps defeat Burr's bid to be governor of New York
	• Burr and Hamilton exchange critical letters in public
	• Hamilton accepts Burr's challenge of a duel at Weehawken, New Jersey, is shot, and dies the next day (July 12)
1854	• Elizabeth dies in New York (November 9)